Memories From My Logbook

A Bush Pilot's Story

Lynn Wyatt

Published by BookLocker.com, Inc., St. Petersburg, Florida.

Printed on acid-free paper.

Booklocker.com, Inc.
2017

First Edition

Table of Contents

The Hummingbird

I wish I could fly like a Hummer; the fact
that I can't is a bummer
No throttle or prop to adjust, just point your
nose and thrust
Refueling in flight is a chuckle, just find a
flower and suckle
No ATC or traffic control, just chirp and
give it a roll
No grounding because of weather, you just
kick back and pluck at a feather
No "cleared to land" required, just sit down
wherever desired
When someone enters your airspace, attack
and give it a good chase
Straight up and around loops and rolls,
flying through trees bushes and polls
Maneuvers beyond belief, then landing on a
leaf
No annual inspections or hundred hours, just
checking flavors of different flowers
No hangar or tie down expenses, just park
on someone's fences
No bi-annual flight review, you always know
what to do
No medical signoff required you can just quit
when you're tired
No rules or regulations, just life joy, and
adulations
What a wonderful sensation—to fly like a
hummingbird.

—By Lynn Wyatt

Chapter 1
Flying the Alcan

April 1976

Lost and alone in a light airplane, low on fuel! Above the Canadian wilderness, jagged mountain tops poked through the cloud layer. I had no clue as to where I was.

I had just bought a new airplane, a Beechcraft Sport 150, but it had to be picked up at the factory. With my 300 hours of flight time, I thought a long cross country trip would be no problem.

I picked up the beautiful, blue-and-gold-on-white airplane from the factory in Liberal, Kansas, with one hour on the tachometer, and took off for Alaska, 3,541 miles away.

Back in April 1976, there was very little controlled airspace, nothing like we have today. There weren't many navigation aids and we didn't have GPS back then. VOR navigation sites did cover most of the United States, but were not available in Canada, at least not available in the part of Canada where I would be flying. There was ADF (Automatic Direction Finder) navigation available, but I didn't have an ADF receiver in my airplane. Which meant I would be flying through Canada using only the chart on my lap and ground reference when I could see the ground.

I landed for fuel in Laramie, Wyoming about mid-afternoon on a very hot day. I fueled the aircraft, ate lunch, and headed out again.

During takeoff, I had used up most of the runway, and the airplane was still not flying or accelerating. Then it hit me—density altitude! With the airport elevation over 7000 feet, the temperature 90 degrees and a density altitude of over 10,000 feet, this airplane only has a service ceiling of 11,650 feet maximum! I almost reached that before leaving the ground.

I pulled the mixture control back about half way to lean the engine, and my baby accelerated and took to the sky, although sluggishly. *I will remember that lesson.*

My plan to follow the Alcan Highway, through Canada, to Alaska, went well until the cloud ceiling over the highway dropped, and visibility fell to zero. I then followed the railroad tracks until the clouds closed in again.

It looked better through a canyon to my left, so I turned in to give it a try. The canyon wound this way and that, and I was finally able to climb above the weather without a clue where I was.

Remember, I was completely IFR (I follow Road/I follow Railroad).

Looking at my chart, I guessed the closest airport was Whitehorse. I located their frequency and called Whitehorse Radio, explaining my situation.

With no navigation aids in Canada in those days, and none indicated on my chart, the guy in Whitehorse said, "Sorry, I can't help you, 'eh."

I explained I was lost, low on fuel, and had no clue what direction to go. The controller told me that Whitehorse had just finished installing a new VOR facility. However, the VOR transmitter had not been commissioned and was legally unusable for navigation. My aircraft had a VOR receiver.

The Whitehorse Radio guy said, "We were just getting ready to test the transmitter," and gave me the frequency. I dialed it in, he "tested" it, and my VOR "off flag" went away. The heading indicator came to life. With the correct heading, I flew directly to Whitehorse, landed, and spent the night drinking abundant amounts of Canadian beer with my new 'Whitehorse radio' buddies. I bought!

My next flight leg was a long one, and after a few hours, I had to pee. I still had about 100 miles to go to reach my destination airport, with no airports in between.

When a pilot has to pee while in an airplane in the middle of the Canadian wilderness, 100 miles to the next airport, that's not good! Getting squirmy, I remembered I had a bottle of water in my survival pack in the back seat. I grabbed the bottle from the pack and poured the water out the little side window. I unstrapped my seat belt, pulled down my pants and uh-oh–the hole in the water bottle was too small for—you know—so now I was ready, and it was even worse! *I have a knife in my survival gear!*

I located the knife and cut an enlarged hole in the bottle. Ah…what a relief! I had filled the bottle to the top and felt better. *Now, what do I do with it?*

I didn't want to pour it out the little window and stain the side of my beautiful blue-gold-and-white airplane. I had to find a place to put it, but it had no cap, I had cut it off. I tried to wedge the bottle upright next to the fuel selector on the floor. It worked for a while until the turbulence hit. I finally had to pick it up and hold it for the next 100 miles until landing.

Another lesson learned: Carry a proper bottle just in case and go easy on the coffee. The rest of the flight was uneventful.

Now that I had made the trip, I was in great demand to ferry airplanes up to Alaska for new owners. They paid me $1,000.00 a trip plus expenses, to fly brand new airplanes from the factory—not too bad!

I made another four trips with a Beechcraft Sundowner, a Sierra, and two Lake amphibious airplanes.

* * *

A memorable event happened on one flight. I had been flying for 15 hours that day and was very tired when I started getting tossed around by a towering cumulus cloud cell.

Cruising at 8500 feet the airplane gradually started to climb. I eased in some nose-down trim, still climbing, pulled back some power, still climbing. Finally, I had the power all the way back to idle. I lowered the flaps and landing gear, pointed the nose down, still climbing, my concern increasing by the second.

Around 14,000 feet the updraft finally spit me out, and I started down. Falling about 1,000 feet per minute. I applied full power, raised the flaps and gear, pulled the nose up, and prayed.

The down drafts finally let go, and I leveled out at 1000ft AGL (above ground level). That was about 9.5 on the pucker meter!

Flying through Mustang Pass I contacted Seattle Approach Control for vectoring to Renton Airport. They vectored me to follow a Cessna 172 and directed me to contact Renton Tower. I contacted Renton Tower and followed the Cessna until I lost him. With the airport in sight, I flew downwind, then turned back toward the runway. On short final, I still had not received a "cleared to land" from Renton. I called the tower and said, "I am on short final for runway 31R".

The tower said, "We don't have a runway 31R". *Oh shit!* I gave it full power and climbed straight out. Moments later I got a call from Renton Tower asking, "Are you a green and white Lake Buccaneer? Boeing Field said one just made a low pass. Don't worry about it. Lots of pilots make the same mistake." They vectored me on to Renton.

Good lesson–way too tired!

* * *

Another flight got a little hairy. I had picked up another Lake Amphibian from the distributor in Tomball, Texas, and was cruising along enjoying the flight when I saw what appeared to be a huge dust storm directly in my flight path which totally obscured visibility. Close to the Midland Airport, I quickly diverted and was cleared for a straight-in approach for landing.

On the approach to landing the dust storm engulfed me and I could barely see the runway lights. I flew the localizer approach on instruments. Then the pitot static ports, which feed data to the instruments, started plugging up with the dust, rain, and mud. This caused my instruments to malfunction, altimeter and airspeed both froze. The storm-tossed my plane around in the turbulence as lightning struck nearby. My localizer was still working, so I was able to maintain runway heading until I made visual contact of the airport. I landed okay and quickly arranged to have the airplane pulled into a hangar. Not long after getting the airplane secured, a big tornado hit just off the end of the airport. It took out the trailer park at the end of the runway.

I had the pitot-static system purged and was on my way the next day.

Chapter 2
Little Yellow Airplane

January 1976

While driving through Anchorage Airport, I spotted this cute little yellow airplane for sale: A Fabric covered Bellanca Citabria 7GCBC, high wing, two-place, tandem seating, with a tail wheel. This plane was fully aerobatic with a 150 HP engine.

I had never flown a tailwheel airplane, but I figured, how tough could it be? I had accumulated around 800 flight hours by then and had attained my commercial, instrument and multi-engine ratings (all in nosewheel airplanes). I figured I was pretty hot stuff. Anyway, I talked to a friend into partnering with me, and we bought the cute little yellow airplane.

I couldn't wait to fly it, but my flying buddies all said, "Never flown a tail dragger huh? You'd better get a check out." Well, even though this was an insult to my piloting skills, I relented and contacted a flight instructor.

I remember telling the instructor, "Tony, I truly don't need you to show me how to fly this thing, but to appease all my buddies, and my partner in this airplane, I agreed to a checkout. I think we can just take her up, once around the flying patch, land, and you can be on your way."

Tony, being a quiet guy, just nodded his head and said, "Okay." He had that look that asked, *"We will soon see if you need a checkout."*

We did our preflight, checked all the controls, springs, wires, struts, tires, prop and oil. All looked good. We strapped in, me in front, Tony in the back, cranked up the engine and started to taxi out. Taxiing immediately started to get interesting. The little airplane had no steering on the ground other than the brakes, and the brakes were little heel pads on the floor, not the toe brakes on the rudder pedals I had always used. To turn the plane, the pilot had to remove his feet from the rudder pedals and push the little pad with his heel on one side or the other to apply the brake and turn the airplane. Ever heard of a ground loop? Well, that's when the airplane spins around in a complete 360-degree circle on the ground. That's what happened on my first turn, barely missing several other parked airplanes on the ramp.

Tony calmly sat there, like he expected this. *He can be such a butt sometimes.* Tony started to explain and demonstrated the finer points of steering the little beast on the ground. After some practice in an open area of the ramp, I started getting it down. *No big deal. This doesn't reflect on my piloting skills. We were still on the ground. How was I supposed to know?*

After another thirty minutes of practice I had it pretty much wired. I contacted Anchorage Tower for permission to taxi for takeoff, and we headed out for the runway. I quickly ran through my CIGAR check: Controls (ailerons, elevator, rudder) Instruments (oil pressure, altimeter set to field elevation) Gas (Fuel selector set to on), Attitude (set trim tabs for takeoff), Run (perform magneto check, carb heat, oil pressure). Checklist complete, *I was sure Tony was impressed.*

I told the tower we were ready to go. We got clearance to pull onto the runway and hold. I pulled out and lined up with the center of the runway and stopped with my two little heel brakes then set the directional gyro to runway heading. Bear in mind, this was Anchorage International Airport. The runways are as wide as some runways are long. It was one of those days with not a breath of wind blowing. *This flight is a waste of time, but I'll make everyone happy and fly around the pattern and finish it.*

8

The tower gave the "cleared for takeoff." I rolled on the power, released the brakes and started moving. As I gained airspeed, I pushed the stick forward to lift the tail. At that moment, everything went to shit! The tail came up and the airplane, all by itself, made a hard left turn, heading for the side of the runway. *What the crap is going on?* I was totally out of control, fighting with the airplane and losing!

Tony calmly said, "I've got it."

He does something, the airplane straightens up, and we lift off. *Holy Moly—that woke me up!*

Tony explained the finer points of "P" factor (engine torque) and its effect on tail wheel airplanes, "When you lift the tail off the runway, it wants to turn left. The proper procedure is to start adding some right rudder, and a little right aileron if required as you raise the tail. This compensates for the torque, and keeps the airplane going straight."

Okay, I get it. A little practice, no problem. That was a close one. Good thing Tony is here.

Once we had convinced the tower that we were okay and didn't damage anything with our almost off-runway excursion, Tony tells the tower, "We have student training in progress."

How humiliating...a "student"...damn, damn, damn.

Once in the air, the airplane flew like all the other planes that I had flown except that it had a joystick (control stick) instead of a control wheel. I flew with my right hand instead of the left, since the throttle and flap controls were on the left. I quickly adjusted to this and found it quite comfortable. The airplane, designed for aerobatics, was light and responsive to control inputs. Visibility was good out both side-windows because one seat was behind the other. *I could get to like this cute little airplane.*

Tony said, "There are two ways to land a tailwheel airplane. The normal way is a three-point landing where you flare above the runway to a pitch angle where all three wheels touch the runway at the same time, just as the airplane stalls. For gusty or crosswind conditions the wheel landing is used. You fly down until the main wheels just touch the runway, then push the stick forward, lifting the tail and holding the wheels on the ground with air loads until you bleed off enough air speed for the tail to come down."

How tough can this be? No problem.

I came around and lined up with the runway; carb heat on, power back, flaps down, airspeed spot on. A textbook approach to landing. *I know Tony must be impressed by my flying skills now, other than that little thing during takeoff...Hey, it's my first time.* We glided down and flared just above the runway in what I believed to be a three point attitude. I figured we were just above the stall when the wheels touched I pulled back on the stick to plant the tail wheel. *Oops! Oh shit! Wrong thing to do.* This nasty little airplane would not stall, and the nose shot back into the air again. I gave a little forward stick to compensate, and the wheels came back down to bounce off the runway and back up again. Forward stick. Bounce. Back stick. Nose up. *What in the hell is wrong with this piece of crap?*

Tony calmly said, "I got it," and he gently landed the airplane.

He is such a smart ass!

Tony suggested we go to a restaurant and discuss a few issues before continuing with our checkout.

Over coffee and many napkin sketches, I started to understand how different the takeoff and landing techniques are between nose wheel and tail wheel airplanes.

Time to try again. This time I brought it in at the same angle, but with a little forward trim dialed in. When the main wheels touched, I released back pressure on the stick and the little yellow airplane landed perfectly.

Now I had my confidence back. I had conquered the little yellow beast and was ready for wheel landings. I knew exactly how to do it, Tony had told me. I lined up on the runway at a slightly higher airspeed and more level pitch angle, I touched the main wheels down on the runway and gave the control stick a hard push forward. Thump, thump, thump—the prop dug into the runway and bent each blade—*Shit! Tony never told me about that part.*

Chapter 3
SKIS

February 1976

I flew the little yellow airplane quite a bit that summer and got to where I could handle the take-offs and landings fairly well on wheels.

As winter moved in, "termination dust" on the higher mountain peaks crept lower each day. Termination dust is the term the old sourdoughs used to describe the snow dusting the mountains tops, announcing the onset of winter—a time to terminate their work and get back to town before they got frozen in.

Each day the snow blanket moved lower down the hillsides until a gossamer covering of white blanketed even the lowest elevations. Lakes and rivers had frozen over and also covered with snow. Bears had settled in their dens for the long winter sleep. Birds had flown south; winter had arrived. A wonderful, beautiful, mystical quiet engulfed the land.

When I originally bought the little yellow airplane, it came with a pair of skis. I moved the airplane to Merrill Field, located across town from Anchorage International. Merrill Field's north/south runway, dedicated to ski airplanes, meant they plowed the runway, parking area, and taxi ways, but a layer of snow and ice remained left in place, so ski operations were still possible. After removing the wheels and installing straight skis, I was ready for a new adventure. At the recommendation of my friends, I called Tony (you remember him) to give me a ski checkout, since I had no experience flying with skis.

As you might imagine, after plowing, snow berms usually two to four feet high, depending on snow fall, bordered the taxiways and runways.

Remember when I mentioned that I steered the little yellow airplane with brakes? Guess what? Skis have no brakes! You steer using the air rudder, by pushing the rudder pedal to deflect the air rudder, then revving up the engine, so the prop blows against the rudder surface, and pushes the tail in the opposite direction you want to go.

We pulled the airplane out of its parking spot by hand and lined it up on the taxiway. I cranked up the engine, added a little power, and off we went. It was going well until coming to my first 90-degree turn. I pushed in lots of power, kicked the rudder pedal hard left. Remember that ground loop I told you about before? Tony calmly pulled the power back and shut down the engine.

We both got out and wrestled the airplane to point in the direction we wanted to go.

Okay, I can do this!

Cranking her up again, off we went. Making little power and rudder inputs back and forth, I was now getting the hang of this pretty well.

Arriving at the runway threshold we held on the taxiway while performing our pre-takeoff checks. Receiving clearance to take the active runway, I pushed in power, kicked the rudder, and ended up high sided and straddling that three-foot berm I mentioned. *Shit!*

Tony called the tower and explained, "There is a student pilot driving the airplane, please be patient with us."
I will get him for this!

After getting out again and freeing the aircraft from its surly bonds, we finally got it pointed down the runway.

The takeoff was uneventful, with a quick mag check on the roll, the airplane got off quickly on the slick, icy runway.

We stayed in the pattern and came around for a few touch-and-go landings. Landing on skis was even easier than landing on wheels. I gently kissed the skis down on the runway, slid for a few feet, added power, and took off again. Making three more perfect touch-and-go landings I determined this was a piece of cake. On my next approach, I informed the tower "This will be a full stop landing."

Flaring the skis inches from the runway, I made another textbook landing! Remember, skis have no brakes! As we slid down the icy runway, it seemed we were speeding up instead of slowing down. *Shit!* The end of the runway approached fast, and, the road ahead had cars crossing! I couldn't get this little yellow 'piece of crap' to stop! *Oh shit...we are going to die!*

Tony calmly said, "I've got it." He pushed in power and took off again. "Tower: student pilot." We went around again.

I'll have to wear my ski mask when I exit the airplane so that no one will recognize me!

Tony then demonstrated a full stop landing. When he touched down, not nearly as smoothly as I did, I might add, he eased the airplane to the side of the runway with less ice and more snow. The increased friction slowed the airplane down. I tried this procedure several times, and it all started coming together.

Now that I could fly this thing on skis, I needed a destination to get out in the wilderness and experience real ski flying. A friend had a cabin on a lake about 50 miles west of Anchorage and asked if I would check it for him, even spend a few days. Hey, no problem! I had an airplane on skis. I could check it out the following weekend and spend a few days relaxing with a good book.

He mentioned he got some very deep snow out there and wanted me to look in on it. He was worried about the heavy snow damaging the roof.

Being the cautious airman that I was, I loaded the airplane with the survival gear required to fly in Alaska — a twelve gauge shotgun, twenty below zero sleeping bag, food, snowshoes, flares, and an emergency locator transmitter (ELT).

All small aircraft that depart or arrive in Anchorage, via Merrill Field or Anchorage International Airport, have to fly across Cook Inlet to Point Mackenzie before turning to the direction they are heading. This allows both control towers to know where everyone should be until they vacate their airspace.

On a wonderfully clear, cold day with unlimited Visibility—we called it "severe clear,"— I climbed over Cook Inlet, and looked out each side of the airplane, verifying the skis and bungees were secure. At about 2,000 feet I settled back for an enjoyable flight when I saw what looked like a black dot straight ahead of me. I was transfixed on this dot for several seconds when I realized it was another airplane coming straight at me.

I slammed the stick full right as fast and hard as I could, almost a reflex reaction. This sweet little yellow aerobatic airplane did a complete roll. As I rolled through 180 degrees upside-down, I saw a Beechcraft Bonanza blast through the airspace that I had occupied a split second before. I don't think this guy ever saw me.

I tried contacting him on the radio to chew him out, but he never answered.

That experience was a full scale on the pucker meter!!!!

Pressing on, the beautiful day brought me back to normal before long. Flying over the Alaskan wilderness in winter is breathtaking, not breathtaking like when you almost center punch a Beech Bonanza and flutter out of the sky in pieces, but breathtaking in a good way.

It took some searching around the area, with everything covered in deep snow, to locate my friend's cabin, until I finally came in for a landing on the pristine snow of the lake. Gently touching down and letting the airplane slow, poof, and darkness. *What the f---?*

Quickly shutting the engine down I assessed my situation. *I'm not underwater, that's a good thing.* The soft powder snow had buried the airplane. *That little shit Tony never told me about this!*

Trying to open the door, I found it would only budge a few inches. Managing to open the window slightly I started to dig away the snow, little by little. I finally got it cleared enough to open the door and climb out. In the deep powder snow, I almost had to swim to reach the top of the snow cover.

The airplane had fallen through, and the wings were resting on the surface. *Holy crap! What do I do now? I can't take off. I can't even start the engine.*

Able to get my snowshoes out of the airplane, I strapped them on, and trudged a deep path to the cabin, while I thought about this unexpected conundrum.

With no radio contact to the outside world and no cell phones back then, I was alone, and not expected back for a few days.

Snowshoeing my way through snow which nearly reached the top of the cabin door, I cleared enough from the doorway to get inside and start a fire. After warming up a bit, I went back outside to clear more snow from my roughly trudged path. Using the snow shovel from the cabin, I cleared around the airplane so I could retrieve my supplies.

The cabin was quite old, built with local logs, and its fireplace made of river rock. The furniture, also made from the local wood, was covered with animal skins. Bear rugs covered the plank flooring and walls, and a moose rack hung over the fireplace. Only one room, the cabin had beds along one wall, a table in the kitchen area, and a couch and chair. A Coleman stove sat on the small counter top for cooking and melting snow for water. The place became very cozy after warming up by the fire and lighting a few candles; the cabin soon took on the pleasant smell of burning pine smoke, hand-hewn logs, home-made furniture, and a wilderness log cabin smell.

Daylight lasted only three to four hours this time of year, and outside it became dark and cold, really cold—like 25-below 0 cold! Inside, the cabin took on an almost surreal slightly smoky look, the fire and candles casting moving shadows around the room and log walls. The fire light reflected off the eyes of the moose head and bear rugs, almost bringing them alive. The only sound, the crackling of the fire.

Inside my toasty warm refuge, I heated a can of beef stew, popped open a bottle of Chardonnay, and settled in for the night with a good book, trying not to worry about that little problem outside.

The next day I spent clearing the heavy snow off the cabin roof for my friend while pondering how to deal with my predicament.

My plan: I would tramp out a runway, using my snowshoes and snow shovel, and create a ramp, where I could drive the airplane to the top of the powder and, hopefully, keep it going.

Getting to work, I was soon sweating inside my fur parka. My beard froze with icicles, and I found it hard to breathe in the extreme cold. I had made a good start on my homemade runway when I had to quit and go inside to warm up. I figured I might finish up the next day and be out of there.

The next morning, after a pot of hot coffee and some bacon and eggs, I was ready to tackle my project again. Using snowshoes and the shovel, I went back to work. Things went well, and in a few hours, I had created a suitable ramp to launch me to the top of the snow.

I also cleared the rest of the snow from around the aircraft. I figured I could accelerate up the ramp and have enough airspeed to keep on top of the powder until takeoff.

Wait until I tell Tony how I handled this situation!

With still enough daylight to get back to town, I loaded my gear and climbed in. *This Alaskan wilderness isn't so tough if you have brains.*

Ready to go, I hit the starter. The prop turned over about half a revolution and stopped. *Oh Shit!* I realazed the engine had frozen from the extreme cold, and so had the battery. *Now what?*

Hauling my gear back to the cabin, I rekindled the fire and tried to figure out my next move. *Aha, I have it.*

Taking the Coleman lantern out to the airplane, I lit it and put it inside the engine compartment, then covered the engine cowling with my "twenty below zero" sleeping bag. The Coleman lantern put out enough heat to warm the engine. Taking the battery to the cabin I put it in front of the fire and got back to my book and copious amounts of Chardonnay.

The next morning, I went out to the airplane, pulled off the sleeping bag and removed the Coleman lantern. The engine was toasty warm, and the paint on the cowling only slightly blistered from the heat. *No big deal.* After reinstalling the battery, the engine fired right up.

Leaving the engine idling and quickly loading my gear, I strapped in and was ready to try my runway ramp. Shoving in full power— the airplane didn't move! *Shit, now what?* Shutting down the engine I jumped out, finding the skis frozen to the snow. Grabbing the wing strut, I rocked the wings up and down, until the skis finally broke free.

Jumping back in, I strapped into the seat belt and harness, re-started the engine, and pushed in full power. The little airplane started accelerating over the hard packed snow up the ramp. When reaching the deep powder I was almost at flying speed, then quickly lifted off. *I had conquered the elements.*

Climbing out over the trees surrounding the lake I settled in for a pleasant flight home. Glancing back inside at the instrument panel I found no flight instrument readings--no altitude, airspeed, directional gyro, nothing! All the instruments were frozen, everything except the whiskey compass, which was almost meaningless at these latitudes. The engine instruments, tach, and oil pressure were working, so I was okay. *Oh well, who needs flight instruments. I know the way home.*

After some time with the cabin heater turned on full blast, the instruments started to come back to life. The rest of the flight was uneventful. Now that was a very educational experience.

My sweet little yellow airplane

Chapter 4
The Lake

April 1977

During the last four years, all my flying had been on wheels or skis, which limited where I could go, considering all the lakes and rivers in Alaska. I decided I needed to get my float rating.

Dean, the dealer for Lake Airplanes in Anchorage, also gave flight instruction. He was always hanging around our FBO (fixed base operator), for free coffee. I got to know him pretty well and decided to get my seaplane rating in the Lake.

The Lake is an extremely cool little airplane: 200 HP fuel injected engine, constant speed prop, retractable landing gear (for water landings) and four seats. The cockpit door/window lifts up and over, allowing you to paddle using a boat oar while steering with your feet using a little water rudder that pops out the bottom of the air rudder. It has an anchor compartment forward of the windscreen, and a cleat to tie it off, like a boat—a very cool airplane indeed.

The engine sits on top of the airplane, aft of the cockpit; the prop pushes from the rear. Wings are aft of the rear seats give passengers unlimited visibility. Throttle, prop, and mixture controls, are located on the cockpit overhead, the landing gear, flaps, and trim are hydraulic. Flaps have only two positions—up or down. There is even an automatic bilge pump in the belly.

What could there be not to love about this sweet little airplane? Wait until your first water landing and then answer.

My first lesson, Dean and I took off from Merrill Field, did a few touch-and-go landings at the airport to get used to the airplane's performance on wheels, which was conventional. Next, air work—stalls, slow flight, steep turns, all standard, even with the engine on top, and a pusher prop. We then flew across Cook Inlet to a nice-sized lake for practice.

Dean demonstrated the first landing. The airplane had no gear warning horn, so I had to say out loud, on every landing, "This is a water landing, the gear is up," or "This is a wheel landing, the gear is down." Dean flew the airplane in—full flaps, prop high pitch, carrying power all the way. He started a slight pitch up, a few inches above the water, and touched down on the step, just aft of the cockpit. He kept flying the airplane, and slowly reduced power to let the airplane settle in. *A piece of cake, I can do that.*

Dean took off with the yoke all the way back and full power. As the airplane started to come on the step, he eased the yoke forward slightly, and the plane flew itself off. *How easy is that?*

My turn—I set up for the approach, announcing, "This is a water landing, the gear is up," prop high pitch, full flaps. I carried the power all the way in, raised the nose slightly. The rest of the landing was a kind of a blur—all sorts of shit happened all at once. I hit the water; the nose went down, then went up, then down. Dean yelled, "I got it." He pulled power off, and pulled the yoke full aft. The nose went up, and the airplane full stalled. We bounced three or four times, then settled in. Dean later explained to me the finer points of porpoising and negative buoyancy.

Dean clarified. "When everything goes to hell on landing, always revert to full stall procedure before things get bad enough to flip the airplane, or rip the wings off." That got my attention!

Well, taking off can't be a problem. I applied full power, holding the yoke full aft, and climbed on the step, while easing the yoke forward to let the airplane accelerate. Thinking it was time to lift off, I pulled back on the yoke. The airplane didn't lift off—it slowed down. I pushed the yoke forward; it sped up. I finally realized, there was a sweet spot in pitch that you have to find, so the airplane could fly off. (Although there *are* ways to trick the airplane off the water before it's ready to fly, but they are not recommended.)

After a few more hours of practice, I received my FAA Seaplane Rating. I took another check ride with the FAA to fly commercially for air taxi operations (FAA part 135 certificate). I now could fly seaplanes/floats for hire.

Liking the versatility of the airplane so much I wanted one for myself. I searched the airports and found an old Lake, (LA4-180), for sale. The airplane had been sitting idle for a long time. It had flat tires, paint peeling, struts sagging, and truly looked rough, but I thought I could fix it.

Contacting the owner, he told me, "The airplane hasn't flown in almost a year, but as far as I know, everything was working when I parked it." I blew up the tires and struts, replaced the battery, changed the oil, gave it a thorough inspection, and got it started. The owner let me take it up for a test flight. Other than cosmetics, most everything worked okay. The engine, overdue it's T.B.O. (time before overhaul), would need to be replaced before long, but that was okay. We agreed on a price, and I bought it.

After flying it around for several months as it was, I decided to rebuild it. I stripped off the paint, acid etched, anodized and painted it. I then installed a new 180 HP engine.

It turned out to be a great little airplane. I flew it all over for hunting, fishing, and just exploring Alaska.

I did have one close call in this airplane. My buddy Ron and I decided to go moose hunting. We planned to fly up the Yetna River, north of Anchorage, land on the river, and taxi onto a small gravel bar, where we would make camp.

We loaded the airplane at Merrill Field—tent, sleeping bags, guns, groceries beer, way too much stuff, and way too heavy. As we departed the airport, I noticed I had to use a lot more aft trim than usual, but thought no more about it. Remember, the wings are aft of the cockpit.

We flew to our spot on the Yenta River, landing downstream, close to the gravel bar. As we slowed down and came off the step, suddenly everything went black, as the nose plunged underwater. Water cascaded over the windscreen, and cabin as we submerged into the brown muddy water.

Holy shit! This never happened before.

Luckily, the engine, located on top, was still out of the water. I shoved in full power, pulled the yoke back, and the airplane shot out of the water like a breaching whale. I kept the power in and drove the airplane onto the beach.

The problem: The heavy load in the cabin was forward of the wings, which put the airplane totally out of CG range. (Center of gravity). I had no idea CG could cause that much effect on the water.

After unloading our heavy, out of balance, cargo, I pushed the airplane back into the river, lowered the landing gear, and taxied onto the gravel bar, where we tied it down.

That was a lesson well-learned the hard way. We were lucky to get out of it with no damage.

We never did see a Moose!

This is the airplane I went under water with

Chapter 5
The Bear Hunt

August 1975

My friend Ron and I planned to go out for a few days' moose hunting. I had a Lake LA-4 200 amphibian airplane at the time, so we set out for my cabin on Shell Lake about 80 miles north of Anchorage. The lake was only accessible by float plane in the summer and ski plane or dogsled in the winter. The Iditarod, Anchorage to Nome, dog sled race ran right past my cabin
.

We set out on an extremely bad day, rain, high winds, and low visibility. We needed to get a special VFR, (visual flight rules) clearance to get out of Anchorage, and then to fly below 500 feet all the way due to the low cloud ceiling.

As we approached the lake for landing, I noticed the tall grass at the approach end of the lake was flattened down in trails, indicating lots of bears in the area. The weather at the lake was even worse than in Anchorage. The wind screamed across the lake, causing white caps and high waves, which made for an interesting landing. We got in okay after a few bounces. The howling wind continued to blow whitecaps and waves over the Plexiglas canopy, almost burying the nose as we taxied to my cabin, where we finally tied down to some trees on the beach.

We thought there were mostly black bears in the area, and decided to take my boat to the end of the lake before dark and maybe get a bear or two. We got our rifles, Ron with a 30.06 using home loaded ammo, and I with my 300 Weatherby Magnum loaded with 220-grain bullets which pumps out 3,158 foot pounds of force at 2,543 feet per second at 100 yards, the ultimate hunting rifle.

Lynn Wyatt

After an extremely wet and bumpy boat ride, we pulled up to the back side of a small spit of land opposite of where I had seen the bear sign. We quietly sneaked through the tall grass, up to a slight hillside, where we could see the river in both directions. We didn't see any bears, so we took a comfortable seat, me in front, and Ron slightly behind. Figuring we had some time to wait, we decided to have a little smoke of Alaska Matanuska Valley's finest weed.

We didn't wait long. Suddenly across the river, about 30 yards away, a huge silver tip grizzly came crashing out of the brush and stopped, staring directly into our eyes. Surprised, I just sat there looking at the monster, when Ron let go with the 30.06, just behind me and to my right. I still hope to recover all my hearing someday. Ron's bullet center punched the bear; it tumbled down the hill to the water's edge—and got up! By this time, I had recovered my senses, so I let it have one with the big Weatherby, and Ron hit him again.

Now the prudent thing to do was wait a while before approaching a bear that appears to be dead. So we waited. After ten minutes, I saw something from the corner of my eye, three more grizzlies were coming up the middle of the stream to catch salmon. It appeared to be a sow and some older cubs. The sow saw us and took off into the tall grass. One cub caught a salmon and followed the first bear. The other cub caught a few more salmon before finally strolling into the tall grass. The grass the bears strolled into was the same grass where Ron and I sat—not a warm fuzzy feeling. We decided to get out of there, but as we turned to leave, we saw two more grizzlies coming down to the stream from the opposite direction.

Not good. I shot one, but only wounded it, and both bears ran into the Alder bushes on the opposite side of the river, the same area where the first grizzly was lying, hopefully dead. The grass

30

was chest high, and a grizzly on all four legs is not chest high so we couldn't see them. The walk back to the boat was traumatic, and that little smoke we had earlier didn't help things in the least!

We got to the boat and took it around the spit, down the river to where the first bear, Ron's, was down. I went over to where I had shot one, finding a blood trail leading into the alders. We decided to deal with the first bear before it got too dark. Tracking a wounded grizzly through tall alders is bad enough without doing it at dusk.

Ron's bear was huge, probably 10 feet tall. Getting dark, we decided to take the bear back to the cabin to skin it. We had cut down some alders for levers and rolled the bear down to the water's edge. Using a couple more alders for ramps, we levered the bear into the boat. It started to rain, and the wind whipped up whitecaps. We almost swamped the boat and returned to the cabin drenched.

Darkness had fallen by the time we finally reached the cabin. We had to skin the bear by lantern light at the edge of the boat because it was too heavy to move further. It felt spooky—dark, rainy, and windy. A bear without its skin resembles a human body, all white and muscled. We needed to dispose of the carcass, as the meat of a grizzly bear is not fit for human consumption. We towed the body out to the middle of the lake, cut it loose and watched it slowly sink out of sight. It gives me the shivers to think about it.

The next day, the weather was still bad, and I had a wounded bear to deal with, not my favorite thing to do. Ron and I headed out in the boat. Ron carried his trusty 30.06 and I had my Smith and Wesson 12 gauge pump shotgun, loaded with a slug/ double 00/slug/double 00/etc. I had eight rounds and figured this was the best choice for close range and thick brush.

We got to the spot where the blood trail started. I could see paths through the grass into the Alders. We followed the trail for a while then lost it. We decided to go in different directions and yell out if we found something. I crawled under the Alders trying to stay on the trail through the grass when I spotted some blood. I put my finger in it. It was still warm. *OH shit!*

The bear stood up, fifteen feet in front of me. That got my attention, and there was no place to go. I let him have one with the 12 gauge, putting a rifled slug dead center in his chest. It just pissed him off, and he let out a screaming growl *I'll never forget.* Time to quit messing around. I started putting rounds through the shotgun faster than I thought possible. After the shotgun was empty, I tossed it down and pulled out my 44 magnum pistol, which I always carried in a shoulder holster for emergencies.

Ron ran up, after hearing my shots. Pumped with adrenaline, I hardly heard him as he shouted, "You got him--put down the 44 mag!"

There was no way we could get this huge bear back to the boat, so we started skinning the hide where I'd shot it. This job took some time, and afterward, we draped the hide over a tree branch that we had cut down to help carry the heavy hide. We trekked back to the boat. After a short distance we found wet fish on our trail still flopping, that obviously another bear had just dropped. We cautiously worked our way back to the boat looking everywhere for more bears.

This place was Grizzly Bear City, and I wanted out of here. Finally, we got the bear skin in the boat and back to the cabin as the weather was getting even worse.

I didn't have a grizzly bear tag, and we had two bear hides to take back. This meant I had to get back to town for a tag before we could transport the hides in the airplane.

The weather had grown much worse by now. Nobody should be flying in this crap. So off I went back to Anchorage. The cloud ceiling had become so low I had to drop down to the Susitna River and fly under the cable car that crossed the cliffs above me to maintain visual contact with the ground and scud run back to Anchorage. Lake Hood had closed, so I snuck in, secretly landing on the back side of the lake.

I went into town and got my bear tag; then went back to the airplane and snuck out of Lake Hood. I battled the weather all the way back to my cabin.

With the Bears properly tagged, we relaxed and waited for better weather for our return.

Me and the Bear and my Airplane.

Chapter 6
Kennecott Glacier Lodge

March 1983

The Kennecott copper mine operated for 27 years extracting $200 million in ore. The mining operation closed in 1938, abandoning everything: dishes on the tables, furniture, wall clocks, mining ledgers, mining equipment—the whole lot. It was like one day they just left, leaving everything behind.

I spent endless hours wandering through the old buildings and exploring the mill site—a fascinating place.

One of the original buildings had been restored to its beautiful original condition and operated as the Kennecott Glacier Lodge. The owner, Liz, invited a few friends and me to buy in with her as partners. She would continue to operate it for us. Liz lived at the lodge full time during the summer season, caring for the guests, with the help of some part-time kids. During the winter, we closed the place, and Liz moved back to Anchorage.

Kennecott is located 235 miles east of Anchorage in the Wrangle Mountains, and 5 miles outside the remote town of McCarthy, population 22.

We had some great adventures, and the flights were beautiful. From Anchorage we flew 119 miles over pristine Prince William Sound, landing in Valdez for fuel and breakfast. Then we flew another 116-mile flight to McCarthy, which had a 3,000 foot gravel runway.

After landing in McCarthy, someone from the lodge met us with our big army surplus deuce- and-a-half truck for the 5 mile trip up the mountain to the lodge. The buildings stood on a hillside facing Kennecott Glacier. Dirt, silt, rocks, and debris that had accumulated over centuries covered the glacier; this is called a glacier moraine.

One evening as we sat on the front porch of the lodge having a chilled glass of chardonnay, the ground rumbled, the building shook, and the moraine shifted, like having an earthquake.

We took the truck down to the face of the glacier to explore for any treasures that might have pushed out the face of the ice. We heard that one time a mastodon tusk was found protruding from the glacier.

The real fun was exploring the old Kennecott mine buildings. Before the area became a national park, we could freely go anywhere.

March of 1983, with the lodge closed for the winter, a mass killing occurred. One of the only two residents of Kennecott, Louis Hastings went over to Chris Richards cabin for morning coffee. As Chris turned to get coffee, Hastings shot him in the head and neck. The shots weren't fatal and Chris grabbed a kitchen knife and slashed Hastings in the leg. Chris ran outside with Hastings shooting at him. He ran to our lodge, to hide inside. Hastings followed the tracks and blood to the lodge. He knew Chris was hiding there, and also knew we had guns inside, so he set the lodge on fire to chase Chris out. Chris managed to flee out the back.

Chris descended a ravine through waist-deep snow in his stocking feet and reached the cabin of McCarthy residents, Tim and Amy Nash. They quickly took him to the runway in McCarthy on their snow machine.

McCarthy, inaccessible by road in the winter, also had no telephone service. A local pilot, seeing Chris needed urgent medical attention, helped him onboard his airplane. He quickly took off and radioed the scheduled mail plane to stay away.

Tim and Amy waited at the runway; Hastings found them hiding there and shot and killed them both.

Two other McCarthy residents, unaware of what happened, came to meet the mail plane. Hastings shot and killed them both as well. He also shot and killed an elderly couple in their McCarthy home. Six people were killed and two wounded, one of who hid by covering up in a snow bank.

The plane with Chris on board flew 100 miles north to Glennallen where they notified State troopers of the shootings. The troopers immediately dispatched their helicopter to McCarthy. They searched the area and found Hastings trying to escaping on a stolen snow machine. He didn't resist arrest. The Troopers then discovered the dead and wounded.

The lodge burned to the ground—with no insurance.

Rather than being sent to a mental hospital, Hastings is serving life in prison.

I never returned.

Lynn Wyatt

Kennecott

Chapter 7
Johnny Mathis

September 1979

Johnny Mathis came to Anchorage for a concert and to experience the "Alaska Adventure." Someone in the entertainment business selected me to fly him out to my cabin on Shell Lake for a wilderness experience. I felt honored to be chosen to spend the day with this legend. I had been listening to Johnny Mathis' music since high school and was thrilled to meet him.

Johnny arrived at my airplane in a big black Cadillac. Stepping out he said, "Hi. I'm John." He then introduced his companions, Gill, his guitarist, and, his secretary.

We strapped into my Lake amphibian for the trip. I kept the airplane parked on the ramp by Big Reds Flying Service. We taxied down the boat ramp into Lake Hood, retracted the landing gear and requested takeoff clearance from Lake Hood Tower. Everyone gets a thrill on their first seaplane takeoff, and they loved it. We climbed over Cook Inlet, then let down to about 200 feet altitude for the flight so we could watch for wildlife along the way. On this warm, sunny, day with clear skies, no turbulence, and not a breath of wind, I kept us low over the winding rivers. We spotted a few bears and moose along the river bank as we headed north, not seeing another person along the way. The remote landscape was always a surprise to first-time visitors.

Forty-five minutes later, we arrived at Shell Lake, its surface shimmering with glassy water, reflecting the surrounding mountains. Touchdown on the reflective surface was like landing on a mirror, with no depth perception.

Watching my vertical speed indicator, I made my approach maintaining 150 feet per minute descent, then eased back to 50 feet per minute, keeping the shoreline in my peripheral vision for reference.

John sat in the front seat. I asked him to watch out the side window and tell me when we were about to touch. He was still watching when we heard the gentle hiss as the hull softly touched the water. "Wow,' he said, "I thought we still had another ten feet to go."

We slowly taxied down the lake with the canopy open. Water gently lapped against the hull as we enjoyed the dreamlike beauty around us. Arriving at my lakefront cabin, I shut everything down, and we stepped out of the airplane, wading to shore in the crystal-clear water. The only noise interrupting the almost total silence were salmon as they wallowed and splashed in the shallows, laying their eggs.

I pulled my boat into the water for our exploration. Our first destination was across the lake to see my friend, Indian Bob and his wife. John seemed to enjoy visiting the bush people in their rustic cabin.

After our visit, we motored down to the stream outlet from the lake enjoying the sights of the unblemished Alaskan wilderness.

Approaching the stream, we could see the salmon so thick you could almost walk on them. John was having a ball out in the river, fishing. Having no luck with the pole, he grabbed a net trying to catch a fish, laughing as he failed then tried again and got soaked in the process. I don't think he ever caught a salmon, but I got a nice one and kept it for our dinner.

Later, back in the cabin, John borrowed some of my extra clothes to wear while his were drying. We all walked about two hundred yards down the shoreline to the lodge, and I introduced John to the little gal that was caretaking the lodge. No other guests were there at the time, and she couldn't believe it was really *Him* (Johnny Mathis,) in the lodge! She got so flustered she could hardly talk, but managed to agree to cook our salmon with some home-grown veggies for our dinner.

The lodge, a one story building made from local logs had a tin roof. It had a sleeping loft above the main floor and a kitchen in back. The girl seated us in front of a long rustic log bar.

After dinner, we all went outside to sit on the dock to enjoy the incredible peace and quiet.

As we walked out, Gill noticed an old guitar leaning against the wall; picked it up and started tuning it. He came outside and started quietly playing. John began to sing one of his incredible ballads. We were the only ones on the lake except for "Indian Bob" and his wife—but they were way across the lake—and out of range.

John's incredibly beautiful and powerful voice echoed through the canyons and across the lake—It was like being in an outdoor cathedral with acoustics from God. I would give anything to have recorded such a magical moment. I'll never forget it!

Unfortunately, even though the days were long with plenty of sunlight, it was getting late and time to go.

While John changed back into his dry clothes, I settled up with the girl at the lodge.

The flight back to Anchorage was even more spectacular. The sun low on the horizon cast shadows that seemed to magnify the beauty around us. A gentle landing on the smooth waters of Lake Hood brought our adventure to a close.

I heard some years later that John was on the Johnny Carson show and remarked that his Alaska Wilderness Trip was the highlight of his tour. I was thrilled that we had made such an impression on this Super Star.

About twenty years later, John still remembered me at a concert in San Diego. He invited my wife and me backstage to see him after he received the note I had dropped off to his stage door manager, asking him to deliver it to John. The note read, "Your Alaska Bush Pilot is here and would like to see you." He sent one of his staff attired in a white tux to our seats with an invitation to come backstage after the show. John welcomed us with smiles and a big hug. The concert was also everything we had hoped it would be!

John is a total gentleman, very gracious and warm; I still think he is one of the greatest singers of our time!

Johnny Mathis trying for a salmon without luck

Chapter 8
Williwaw

October 1979

Williwaw: a sudden violent squall blowing offshore from a mountainous coast.

My hand-held radio alerted me to a call from Anchorage airport security asking me to contact them. I was busy doing my real job at Flying Tigers airline as an Aircraft mechanic with two 747's on the ground that had problems. I gave them a quick return call. They advised me that my airplane had received a little damage at its tie-down location and I should come down when available. I explained I was too busy at the moment, but would swing by later. I was no way prepared for what I would find...

A few hours later after our 747's had dispatched, I drove the company pickup truck to my tie-down on the airport next to Big Reds. I expected that someone had bumped a wing tip or something minor.

My airplane had been tied down with three ropes: The tail, and both wings. The flight control yoke was tied back and left with the seat belt.

Instead I found this!

A williwaw had come through during the night, ripping out all my tie-downs and flipping the airplane up and over. My airplane tore the tail section off a Cessna 185 parked next to me and landed upside down on top of a Cessna 206, completely cutting the tail section off my airplane.

I could not believe it. The guy on the radio had said "a little damage". What the hell would he call *big* damage?

I loved this airplane. I had picked it up new at the factory in Texas and flown it to Alaska.

Fortunately, I had insurance. The airplane was totaled, and I was paid enough to buy a used Cessna 185. I bought the wreckage from the insurance company, removed all the radio communications and navigation equipment for installation in the 185, and sold the wreckage.

The wrecked airplane is flying again after being rebuilt.

Chapter 9
Big Red's

May 1980

After having just purchased a Cessna 185 equipped with floats, wheels, and skis, I was looking for a slip on Lake Hood to park it on floats. What an experience this would turn out to be...

The Cessna purchase came as a result of my previous airplane, a Lake LA-4 200, which was destroyed in a freak wind storm while tied down at Lake Hood.

Lake Hood is the largest floatplane base in the world and it has a long waiting list for tie-down slips. Finding a classified ad that Big Red's Air Taxi Service had a tie-down slip for lease on their dock, I jumped at the opportunity.

Big Red's was one of a dozen Air Taxi Operators based on Lake Hood at the time.

The operation consisted of an old red and white checkered wooden building, ten feet wide by twenty feet long, on the lake shore with a dock that could park five floatplanes, if you carefully squeezed them in.

The building consisted of a small office with a counter separating it from the reception area, which had a couch, table, and a few chairs. Piles of Alaskan hunting and fishing magazines littered the table top.

Big Red's was a partnership consisting of four old ex-military buddies: Bill, a nice Mormon guy with a Cessna 185, and Dave and Paul, partners in an old battered Cessna 206. Dave did the flying and Paul did the aircraft maintenance, which was considerable.

The last partner, Gary, owned a Cessna 206 on wheels with big tundra tires, usually parked on the gravel in front of the office. Gary, the stability in the group, kept things running smoothly, including the bookkeeping, contracts, and financing.

Dave and Gary also flew C130's for the Alaska Air National Guard. Gary's real job was an airline pilot. I think Paul was also a mechanic for the Guard.

Bill worked full time at Big Reds; everyone else was just part-timing it for fun.

The guys asked if I'd like to join their motley crew, and buy a share of the partnership, which I did.

We all drummed up our own business and flew our own airplanes under the Big Red's Air Taxi certificate. This gave us write-offs for the airplanes, fuel, maintenance, etc., which was the idea, as we were all working other full-time jobs. Except for Bill.

Let me tell you about Bill. Bill, in his mid-thirties, a nice looking guy, in a Gomer Pyle sort of way, always friendly, would do anything for anyone—you know the kind. Bill's problem was that he seemed to have a black cloud over his head most of the time.

I recall the time we had engine starting problems. My engine started acting up first. It took several clicks of the starter before engaging and turning the engine over. The next day I replaced the starter solenoid—end of problem.

Bill started having the same problem with his engine. I told him the easy fix, but Bill, the procrastinator, kept putting it off until one day, after dropping off passengers at one of our fishing cabins on a small lake, his airplane wouldn't start.

Bill decided to prop it by hand. He carefully tied a rope to the tail strut, where the tail wheel goes, when the airplane is on wheels, not on floats. The other end he tied to a tree. He set the throttle to about half power and primed the engine. He walked on the float, around the open cockpit door, to reach the prop.

He pulled the prop through, and the big 300HP engine roared to life. Bill smiled as he walked around the open door to the cockpit. That's when the rope slipped off the tail wheel strut. The airplane lunged forward, and the door knocked Bill off the float and into the lake.

Remember, he had set the throttle to half power. The airplane accelerated, came up on the step, and proceeded to go into a left turn, caused by P-factor (engine torque). Bill, stood waist-deep in the lake, watching all this when he realized the airplane was making a full circle and coming right back at him.

He dove under the near-freezing water as the airplane passed over his head. The plane continued up onto the bank, and into the trees off the end of the lake, ripping the wings off, and completely messed up a perfectly good airplane.

We all knew where Bill had gone, so when he didn't return, we flew out to his location, found him, and what remained of his airplane.

We hired a helicopter (at great expense) and brought the aircraft and wings separately back to Anchorage.

49

Bill, not a licensed mechanic, decided he could fix the airplane himself. He ordered a set of wings from "Trade-a-Plane," a few other bits and pieces, and started to work. This reconstruction project was being done right in front of our office on the gravel. Not good advertising! Bill also removed the fuel control for overhaul while he was at it—a Bad idea.

He carefully covered the intake manifold with rags to keep dust out with the fuel control removed for overhaul. Weeks later, with used wings installed, a new prop, and overhauled fuel control, the airplane, now on wheels, was ready to be tested.

Bill taxied to the dirt strip off the end of Lake Hood for the test flight. At full power, he roared down the runway and lifted off. All was going well until the engine quit—remember those rags in the intake to keep the dust out? He missed one.

Okay, he would just put back down on the remainder of the dirt strip. He landed just fine but ran out of runway. There was a big ditch off the end of the strip. The main wheels went into the ditch, flipping the airplane onto its back and partially ripping the wings off—again.

Summer was our busiest time of the year, and losing an airplane was certainly going to hurt, but we figured the rest of us could take up the slack.

We told Bill he should just watch the office and stay out of the airplanes for a while. He humbly agreed and did quite well, until one day a group of Alaskan Indians came into the office.

They needed to charter a flight to their village. The landing would have to be on the beach near King Salmon. And, they had cash.

Memories From My Log Book: A Bush Pilot's Story

The rest of us were away on flights. Bill, being the only one around, spotted Gary's Cessna 206, with the big tundra tires, parked out front of the office. He locked up the office, loaded up the Indians and off they went to King Salmon.

Bill was determined to redeem himself with this "cash deal." He located a long clear stretch of beach near the Indians' village. He made a careful approach and gently touched down on the beach. All went well until the nose wheel found a wet soft spot in the sand. Over the airplane slowly went, landing on its back. Thankfully, no one was hurt. After careful examination of the airplane, Bill determined there was almost no damage. He hiked up to the village to get some of the natives to help him turn the airplane over so that he could fly back to Anchorage. "Maybe no one would know about this one." It took him some time to round up a few helpful bodies and get back to the beach.

As Bill came over the last hill back to the beach, he looked down. "Guess what?" The tide had come in. The only parts visible of the overturned airplane were the nice big tundra tires sticking up out of the water.

We didn't let Bill fly again that season...

Note—That's me in the brown jacket with my airplane behind me parked on the lake. The other guy is Bill. *Gotta love him!*

Chapter 10
Northern Lights

February 1980

Winter is a magical time to fly in Alaska. The sun rises around 10:00 a.m. and sets around 2:00 p.m. All lakes and streams frozen and snow covers everything in an endless blanket of white, giving an almost surreal quiet that makes you want to whisper, so as not to disturb your surroundings.

On clear nights, when the moon is out, reflections off the snow give good ground visibility, even in remote areas with no lights. However, on nights with no moonlight, it can be blacker than the inside of a cow, making for dangerous flight conditions.

I had planned to fly my Cessna 185, equipped with straight skis, no wheels, out to my cabin on Shell Lake, for a restful weekend with a good book, and a visit with old friends.

On a glorious, bright, cold, moonlit, morning I untied my aircraft from the ice on Lake Hood, next to Anchorage International Airport.

Lake Hood is the largest seaplane base in the world, having a landing channel and a separate taxi channel heading east /west and a shorter landing channel heading north/ south. Most of the bush pilot services operated from Lake Hood, in addition to several hundred private airplanes.

In winter, many of the float planes were just pulled up on the bank, securely tied down until breakup (local term for when the ice melts). Those who wanted to fly through the winter had to remove floats and install skis.

The standard procedure to create tie-downs for the planes in winter was to auger a hole in the ice, drop a rope tied to a short piece of 2X4 through the hole, let it freeze for about five minutes, and you had a secure tie down until breakup.

Running electrical cords from our office out to the airplane, I installed heaters, one in the engine compartment, one in the cockpit to keep the instruments from freezing and the engine warm enough to start in the below freezing temperatures.

Protective covers were installed over the engine cowling, wings, windshield and tail section for easy removal of snow, ice or frost buildup.

Arriving at my tie-down early I prepared to fly out to see some friends on Shell Lake.

After loading my survival gear, supplies, groceries and mail for my friends, I removed the covers, heaters, electrical cords and tie downs, then performed the preflight inspection. Everything looked good. I was ready to go. Before climbing in, I had to rock the wings to break the skis loose from the ice.

A quick shot of primer and the engine fired up with a throaty roar. I loved the sound of that big powerful Continental IO-520, 300 horsepower six-cylinder engine.

Making contact with Lake Hood tower, co-located in Anchorage International tower, I requested clearance for taxi.

One side of the tower controls the big 747 and DC-10 airliners that come and go from exotic points around the world, stopping for fuel before continuing to their far away destinations. The other side of the tower controls bush airplanes bound for the Alaska wilderness.

Receiving clearance I taxied down the bumpy ice to the takeoff area. The skis made a pleasant scraping sound as they slid across the ice and frozen snow.

The airplane felt light, with only me and minimal supplies I needed to take out to my friends. Using the air rudder and a burst of power I swung the airplane around to the take-off direction. With the engine gauges all in the green, propeller in climb position, fuel selected to both tanks, flaps up, trim set, cowl flaps open, DG set, I was ready to go.

The control tower cleared me for takeoff. I pushed in the throttle, feeling my adrenaline rush as the big engine roared to power. The airplane shot ahead like it couldn't wait to take to the sky. I did a quick magneto check on the roll. It seemed I barely had the throttle pushed in and was airborne in the still cold air.

The 185 climbed effortlessly in the below-freezing temperature. I pulled the throttle and prop back to climb power as the airplane continued to accelerate. Feelings of pure exhilaration and joy nearly overpowered me as I pulled the airplane into an almost vertical climb before leveling off. *Almost better than sex—Almost!*

Thirty minutes later, as dawn broke over the horizon, lighting up the magnificent splendor around me, I buzzed over my friend's cabin to let them know I was there, then came around, lining up for an approach to the lake. No runway to line up with, no wind, I just pointed the nose for a straight-in landing next to my cabin, across the lake from my friends.

Pre-landing check: cowl flaps closed, power back, prop high pitch, wing flaps 20 degrees, fuel on both, airspeed 60 knots, I lowered the nose and let the airplane descend, then gently touched down, skis shushing on the pristine snow. I added a little power and taxied up in front of my cabin.

It was always a surreal feeling going out to my cabin after a long absence, and this was my first flight here this winter.

After shutting down the engine, I sat there taking it all in. My little red cabin, almost covered in snow. There was total silence, except for the crackling of my aircraft engine cooling down.

Here I was, at my own cabin, in my own airplane, in the wilderness of Alaska. A far cry from that "born and raised" California boy. *It just doesn't get much better than this.*

I hauled the gear up to my cabin and fired up the earth stove that I always left full of wood and ready to light in the case of emergency.

While the cabin warmed up, I left to secure the airplane. I put on the wing covers just in case it snowed. When finished, I returned to the toasty warm cabin.

I had built the cabin the previous year with the help of some good friends. One room, about 30 by 30 feet, with the kitchen in the rear, bunk beds along the side wall, and a living room with a couch and chairs up front.

Because the walls and ceiling were heavily insulated, the big Earth Stove in the center of the room could run you outside, even in the coldest temperatures, if you got it too hot.

The top of the earth stove was also great for cooking and more fun than using the Coleman stove on the kitchen counter. Windows in front overlooked the lake, and a deck ran around the front and sides, with stairs leading down to the lake fifteen feet below.

Invited to join my friends, Indian Bob and his wife for dinner, I also brought their supplies and mail. They lived in a log cabin about 300 yards away on the opposite side of the lake.

I didn't know what kind of Indian Bob was. He was a big man, about two hundred fifty pounds, with long greasy black hair past his shoulders, and a "Fu Man Chu" mustache. He rolled his own cigarettes, not all tobacco, and chain-smoked.

He never told me about his background, and I never asked. Lots of people move to the wilderness to escape or get away from something they don't want to share. It's best just not to ask.

When I came out of my cabin later that day, it was pitch black, with no moon and no reflected light off the snow. As I looked up at the sky, there were more stars visible than I could ever have imagined.

I strapped on my snowshoes and started across the lake, guided by the light from Indian Bob's cabin, the temperature, a brisk 20 below 0, the sky, crystal clear.

All was deathly quiet. Only the crunch of my snowshoes on the crispy snow and the sound of my breathing through a heavy scarf disturbed the wonderful sound of silence.

Suddenly the sky lit up like it was on fire, a weaving gossamer curtain of red, blue, green and pink. The lights undulated like a sensuous dancer behind silken robes. I was mesmerized by the display. Beyond comprehension!

Later, I read that it could not be, but I swear, I could hear the lights crackle as they swayed in the sky.

Awestruck at the unbelievable beauty happening before my eyes, I had no words adequate enough to describe what I witnessed that night.

This display could only be by the hand of God, as no man could create such beauty!

I have seen the Northern Lights (Aurora Borealis) many times since then, but nothing to equal that night.

As I reached Indian Bob's cabin, I called them outside. We all sat around the porch watching until the display went away as quickly as it had begun.

Bob's cabin, built entirely by him and his wife, was made from rough-hewn logs from the local hillside. Inside, it felt like a step back in time—no electricity—the only light from candles and hurricane lamps, and the heat from an Earth Stove, which they also used for cooking.

They kept the meat stored in a catch behind the cabin. The catch is a small shed (freezer) on stilts to keep the animals from robbing the meat. Bob wrapped pieces of tin, from old cans, around each of the legs so animals couldn't climb up to the meat.

Remote cabins in the bush all seemed to have a common unique smell. Not unpleasant, but different. A combination of infrequent bathing, animal hides, open fire, candles, and Cooking—a cozy smell of honest hard labor with no frills, a handmade shelter, like the den of a bear, or fox—a place built to survive the harsh Alaska wilderness.

After a great dinner of moose meat, beans and a nice bottle of Chardonnay I had brought for the evening, we chatted about worldly events, the latest gossip and the upcoming Iditarod sled dog race, which passed about 200 yards from the lake. We talked about the quantity of local game, and how Bob was doing on his trap lines. It's such a completely different, laid-back lifestyle out in the bush; you can almost feel your pulse slow down as you put away the stress of city life, traffic, noise, and crowds. You think only of basics.

Getting back to my cabin was somewhat more difficult. I hadn't thought to leave a lantern burning. I couldn't find my cabin in the pitch black night. I set off in the general direction, stumbling around for about 45 minutes, I followed the shoreline until I ran into my airplane parked in front of my cabin. Chilled to the bone, I finally reached the warmth of my cabin.

Altogether it was a wonderful day.

Me and my Cessna 185 outside my cabin on Shell

Lake

Northern Lights (Aurora Borealis)

Chapter 11
Stony River

August 1980

A local big game guide, Hoppy, hired me to fly hunters and supplies to his hunting camps in the Wrangle Mountains. My flights were from Anchorage to Two Lakes, via Merrill Pass, using my Cessna 185 float plane. The beginning of another great adventure.

Hoppy met me at Two Lakes with his Super Cub on tundra tires. He used a tiny, sandy beach at the head of the lake for landing. We transferred supplies and passenger from my Cessna to the Cub. He flew the load to his spike camp, on the Stony River, landing on a tiny gravel bar. The useful load of the Cessna 185 on floats is 1600 pounds, including passengers, cargo, and fuel. The Cub needed to make three to four trips to haul everything I carried in one load. The Cub could only carry one passenger and supplies each flight.

When the weather closed in, and we couldn't meet at the prearranged time, I stayed the night in a friend's log cabin near the sandy beach, hoping we could rendezvous the next day.

With the season in full swing, I made several trips a week, hauling in supplies, fresh hunters, and gear. Hoppy usually met me with hunters returning from camp for the trip back to Anchorage. These guys were tired, dirty, unshaven, and smelly, but usually thrilled with their experience. They usually had their trophies: moose racks, bighorn sheep heads, hides and meat, and grizzly bear hides. These guys paid big bucks for a grand slam hunt: moose, bear *and* bighorn sheep.

* * *

I arrived at the lake early one sunny, crystal-clear day, not another human within miles. Salmon splashed and flopped around in the shallow waters, while several eagles feasted down the beach. The snowcapped Neacola Mountains brightly reflected in the mirror-like lake.

I thought how truly blessed I was to experience the magnificent beauty of a place few people will ever see while flying a float plane in this wonderful wilderness—and getting paid for it.

However, even while enraptured by the serenity and beauty around me, my eyes still kept looking back towards the pass, searching for telltale signs that weather was moving in, closing the door of the pass. Alaska weather is extremely fickle; it can change in the blink of an eye from a sunny, warm day to snow.

The Cub coming over the mountain interrupted my reverie. Soon I saw Hoppy gliding over the Alders, and lightly touching down on the beach; the big tundra tires seemed to float on top of the sand.

Hoppy was a big man, six foot two, 250 pounds, a dentist in Anchorage during winter months. Quiet, soft-spoken, almost bashful, he turned into the epitome of a mountain man during hunting season.

I remember him crashing through the brush, a huge set of moose antlers across his shoulders, 150 pounds of moose hindquarter strapped to his back. He wore a red, torn flannel shirt, a 44 magnum pistol hanging from a shoulder holster, jeans, rubber boots, and a white cowboy hat. The mild-mannered dentist had transformed into "Jim Bridger, Mountain Man!"

The game, so plentiful back then, the hunters who remained long enough, usually got their trophies. Several hunters simply gave up early, unable to adjust to the extreme Alaskan outback, and went home.

Most of our clients came from Germany for the big Alaskan trophies. Many spoke no English, which proved extremely difficult at times.

An unusual amount of rain this year, caused the Stony River to rise, covering the gravel bar Hoppy was using for landing. He had to land his Cub on the tundra several hundred yards from camp. He said, "If you think you're good enough, you can try to land the Cessna on the Stony River."

He flew me over in the Piper Cub to check it out.

A straight stretch of river about 75 to a 100 yards long looked useable. It required taking off and landing around a bend in the river, which shouldn't be a problem. The riverbank, just slightly wider than my wing tips, meant I had to nail it, right down the middle. I thought I could do it.

I came in, low and slow to check things out. It looked pretty good. Coming around again, I set up for landing. My first attempt, I was a little fast and high. Full power, I went around to try again. This time, I put down full flaps and carried lots of power, holding 50 knots airspeed (just above stall speed.) I passed over the tight bend in the river, lining up on the longer, slightly straighter section. Barely clearing the river bank on approach, I touched down on the right float, pulled off the power, dumped the flaps, and hauled back on the yoke while continuing around the corner.

A piece of cake! Why are my hands shaking like this? I must admit, that landing was right up there on the pucker meter! *Now I have all week to worry about taking off from here.*

In camp, the main cooking tent included a gourmet cook (at least the cook thought so) by the name of Hal. Nearby a meat-drying tent with screened sides let the air flow through, to keep flies and bugs out. Sleeping tents were set up away from the cook and meat tents, as a precaution against nocturnal visits from four-legged friends attracted to the smells. A sauna had been dug into the hillside, next to the river. Overall, it looked like a nice place to stay for a few days.

I had my Assistant Guide License, so I stayed for the week, leading hunters on day hunts. (Non-residents are required to have a guide.) After a few days of hunting, I found I didn't have the killer instinct to shoot harmless animals; bears are not harmless. Alone one evening, I staked out a nearby meadow. A huge moose with the biggest rack I have ever seen wandered out of the trees. He had his eyes on a lady moose across the meadow and paid no attention to me. As I aimed my 300 Weatherby Magnum wide angle scope on this magnificent creature, he filled the scope I just couldn't do it. Wishing him good luck with his new moose-lady friend, I wandered back to camp. I didn't dare mention the moose to the guys in camp; they would have been on him as quick as a hobo on a ham sandwich!

Time for me to get back to town. The river was going down more each day, giving me less water for takeoff. I had to take Hal, the cook, and his gear with me, but still needed to keep the airplane as light as possible for a short takeoff.

We taxied downriver as far as we could, until we ran out of water. We had to maneuver around the exposed gravel bars. Some spots, too shallow to taxi over with our body weight onboard, forced us to jump out and drag the airplane to deeper water. I hoped we would clear these spots when we were on the step during our takeoff run.

Jumping out again onto the river bank, we pulled the wings around to get the airplane lined up for takeoff. Just as we started our take-off run, a large piece of driftwood came around the bend, tangling up the water rudders. I pulled the power back as Hal jumped out on the float to free us. Unfortunately, more driftwood was coming. We had to get out *now!*

I kept the airplane from drifting downstream, using engine power. Hal jumped back in as I firewalled the throttle, putting down 10 degrees of flaps to get on the step as quickly as possible. We started accelerating upstream on rapid, shallow water. The plane came up on the step very fast. I heard the keels of the floats hitting and dragging across the gravel and shallow spots, and the wing tips clipping the overlying brush along the river bank. Driftwood bounced off the floats; I had no room to maneuver. This takeoff felt over the top, hairy. My adrenaline was in full flow. This whole takeoff could go to shit in a heartbeat if I made the slightest screw-up. Rolling one float out of the water while going around the bend, I grabbed another notch of flaps and yanked the airplane off the water just before a large gravel bar. I lowered the nose to gain airspeed and followed the river upstream until I was finally able to climb above the river and trees.

Whew! I wouldn't want to do that every day. Glad I brought an extra pair of shorts!

A few minutes later we landed at Two Lakes. After a thorough check of the airplane for any damage resulting from our harrowing Stony River takeoff, everything seemed okay except for Hal, who was still shaking.

Hoppy met us at Two Lakes with meat and trophies to haul back to Anchorage. Able to use the gravel bar again, he made another four trips in the Cub. Hal and I loaded everything in the Cessna.

Even though we loaded the Cessna to the maximum, plus some, I wasn't worried, as we had three miles of Two Lakes for takeoff.

The moose racks, too big to fit inside the airplane, had to be tied outside on the float struts.

We filled both float compartments and cabin with moose meat, hides, and gear. The airplane was so heavy the top of the floats were almost under water. (That was our weight and balance check back then.) If the float tops were above water, relatively level, we were probably good to go. Surprisingly this worked pretty well.

Idling out onto the lake, I performed the requisite checklist from memory: flight controls free, wing flaps up, cowl flaps open, and trim set for takeoff, altimeter set to Lake elevation, DG (directional gyro) set to the mag compass heading, and fuel selector to both tanks. I set the radio to emergency frequency 121.5. We monitored this frequency to receive any ELT, emergency locator transmitter, signals that automatically transmitted from a crashed aircraft, or switched on for help.

Running the engine up to 1700 rpm, I cycled the prop several times, checked the mags, oil pressure, CHT (cylinder head temp,) suction gauge, amp meter, and set the mixture to best EGT (exhaust gas temp.) Checklist complete.

Retracting the water rudders, I applied full power while pulling back the yoke, and was quickly on the step, then

going—and going—and going. The airplane wou
heavy, and the cylinder head temp was nearing the na

I pulled back the power, coming off the step, water splashing
up the sides as we settled back in the lake. Taxiing back to the
beach, we off-loaded about fifty pounds of gear, while the engine
cooled down. I could retrieve the gear on my next trip.

The next takeoff, I made a wide turn, crossing over my wake I
pulled the flaps down, and we were airborne—barely. Several
more miles in ground effect, with the gentle coaxing of the flight
controls, we finally started to gain airspeed and altitude. I set climb
power of 25 inches manifold pressure, and 2500 rpm. Hal let out a
sigh of relief.

Leveling off at 5000 feet altitude, I set the power to cruise, 22
inches, 2200 rpm and leaned the mixture to best EGT to conserve
fuel.

We then entered Merrill Pass, approximately twenty-five
miles long, lined on both sides with towering snowcapped
mountains. A very narrow section, about halfway into the pass at
3300 feet elevation, requires an immediate ninety-degree turn to
prevent running into a towering glacial- topped vertical wall of
mountain, a mistake many pilots didn't live to talk about.

As we passed through the narrow section, the air temperature
started to drop, and it began to snow. Visibility dropped to almost
zero, and the airframe was picking up ice. The windscreen
remained clear for a while with defrosters on full, but then started
to collect ice and fog up, except for a small six-inch circle above
the defroster.

Freezing rain, ice, and snow began to accumulate on the wing
struts and floats. We were so heavily loaded the airplane couldn't

take much more weight. I flipped on the pitot heat to keep ice from plugging up my airspeed intake source and selected the alternate static source for altimeter and vertical speed indicators. Ice on the fuselage can block the static ports giving erroneous readings.

The controls began to feel sluggish with the additional weight, and I had a hard time holding altitude. I concentrated flying as smoothly as possible, with no sudden control changes, while as I pushed the throttle and prop back to climb power, trying to maintain altitude.

I saw the ground close below and vertical cliffs on each side, but there was almost zero forward visibility. I was committed. I had to continue straight ahead, using all my skills to keep the airplane from stalling and plunging to the rocks below.

Finally, after about ten miles, the temp started to warm up. The windscreen cleared and ice from the wing struts started to melt and fly off in chunks. I saw Lake Chakachamna ahead. We were through the pass

Once through the mountains, the snow stopped and visibility cleared completely. Reaching Cook Inlet, I needed a break from almost squeezing the juice out of the controls, so I let Hal fly us along the coastline back to Anchorage, about sixty miles, where I took control again for landing at Lake Hood.

Hal had radioed ahead for a taxidermist and meat packer to meet us on arrival and haul away our bounty. They were amazed this little airplane could haul such a load, but hey…this is Alaska. That's what we do.

Merrill Pass is so treacherous most pilots refuse to fly through it, even in good weather. Fifteen crashed airplanes are still littering the pass at last count.

I made thirty-four more trips through the pass that season, not all as pleasant as this one.

My Cessna 185 I flew to the Stony River

Chapter 12
Thin Ice

May 1980

With summer fast approaching the days were getting longer and warmer. The airplanes, still on skis, would have to be pulled off the ice before long and changed over to floats for the summer.

A family that lived in the bush contacted me for a ride home to their cabin, located on a lake about 50 miles north of Anchorage. They arrived at the airplane with a massive load of gear: two adults, two kids, two sled dogs, groceries, luggage, boat parts, outboard motor, guns, and everything else needed to survive a summer in the bush.

After numerous tries and rearranging, we finally squeezed everything on board. We packed the airplane to the ceiling, maxed out, more than slightly over gross weight. During takeoff, it took most of the lake to get the airplane off and flying, but with the cold air and slick ice for a runway, we finally made it.

Arriving at their lake, the first thing I noticed was one end of it had already thawed, leaving a large patch of open water. Not good. I worried about the condition of the remaining ice. I flew around the lake several times, looking for the best place to land. The passengers assured me it was always like this at this time of year, and not to worry. *Right, I've heard that one before!*

Using the bush pilot procedures for checking unknown ice conditions before landing, I kept the airplane light--just dragging the skis through the snow and ice, then taking off again. I came around, looking at the ski tracks for any evidence of water filling in. Any water indicates the ice is too thin and dangerous for ing. The ice looked solid, no water. I came around again and ₊ched down as gently as possible.

Everything went well until I slowed down almost to a stop. That's when the tail of the heavily loaded airplane fell through the ice.

The tail wheel and lower fuselage broke through, with the horizontal stabilizers lying flat on the ice holding the tail section from sinking further. The ski tips were pointing up at an extreme angle. I was scared shitless the ice would give way, and the airplane would sink through the slush.

Jumping out of the airplane, I frantically started to drag passengers and freight out as quickly as possible, to lighten the load. The day warmed up by the minute under the bright sunlight. I hastily got everyone and everything out, scattering their gear in piles around the sinking airplane.

I instructed the two adults to get behind the wing struts, one on each side, and push with everything they had, once I powered up the engine. When, and if, the airplane started to move, they were to jump out of the way, so the tail didn't run them over.

Firing up the big 300 HP engine, I gave it full power. The airplane shook, vibrated and rocked, but didn't move. I yelled, "Push harder!" They leaned into it, and the airplane finally started to crawl forward, as the pushers jumped out of the way.

The skis and tail popped up on the ice, and the airplane accelerated. I felt the ice crack and give way as I gained speed for takeoff. Without the heavy load onboard I was quickly airborne —lesson learned!

****

I am reminded of the story of a guy that chartered a flight to his cabin in the summer. He wanted the pilot to fly him to his cabin, pick up some gear, then fly him back out.

As the pilot flew over the lake of intended landing, he commented to his passenger, "That lake looks too short for me to take off again if I land." The passenger said, "Old what's-His-Name (another bush pilot on Lake Hood,) flew me in and out last year." The pilot, not to be outdone by another pilot, landed.

Once on the lake, it looked even shorter. When the passenger got back on board, the pilot expressed his concerns. The passenger told him "Old what's-His-Name, did it last year."

This pilot knew he was as good, if not better than, Old what's-His-Name, so he figured he could do it.

He taxied to the farthest point on the lake and gave it full power. Once the floats came on the step, he made a turnaround the lake while accelerating. Crossing his wake, he pulled on the flaps and lifted into the air. He gave the airplane everything it had. He just cleared the tall trees off the end of the lake, but only made it about another 50 feet before stalling out and crashing into the trees.

"Shit!" the pilot said, feeling somewhat inadequate in his flying abilities.

The passenger said, "You shouldn't feel too bad. "Old what's-His-Name, only made it about 10 feet past the big trees!"

Never trust the passenger!

The airplane I fell through the ice

Chapter 13
Whittier

September 1980

A group of hunters hired me to fly them to an area on Prince William Sound. The trip required flying through Portage Pass, breathtakingly stunning on clear days, treacherous in bad weather when clouds obscure the terrain. Some pilots tried to get through in marginal conditions and never made it.

We observed several wrecks on the way through the pass before flying over Prince William Sound and the town of Whittier. The beauty of the sound is almost beyond description: 3,800 miles of coastline with crystal clear waters, glaciers of turquoise ice meandering like placid highways through the mountains down to the water's edge; pristine beaches, fjords branching off in all directions; rain forests of Sitka spruce and western hemlock outline the beaches. The Sound contains 150 glaciers dramatically calving huge chunks of ice into the sea.

Thirty minutes later, I began letting down to our destination, landing on the crystal-clear waters of the Sound. I cut the engine and glided up to a primeval white sandy beach; the quiet felt almost deafening.

After unloading passengers and gear, we made arrangements for a pick-up in five days, weather permitting. Wading into the water with my hip boots pulled up, I turned the airplane around, pulling the heels of the floats onto the beach. Firing up the still warm engine, I taxied out a few yards, pointed the aircraft into the wind, applied full power, and was off in seconds heading back to Anchorage.

The weather was deteriorating, but still flyable when I reached the pass. I flew close to the right side in case someone was coming from the other direction; it also gave me room to make a 180 degree turn if needed. I needed! The pass was socked in—zero visibility. I rolled hard over into a steep turn. On instruments, I entered the cloud for a few seconds before breaking out. *Whew...that got my attention!*

I turned back towards Whittier and landed in the bay. I tied up to the boat dock and waited for the weather to clear. After a few hours, staring at the pass, I realized it wasn't going to clear up today; I was weathered in!

I secured the airplane to the dock with a few extra lines as it gently rose and fell with the ocean swells, water lapping at the floats. I grabbed my overnight gear, which I always carried for situations like this, and went up to the hotel.

Whittier has only one building in town, an old fourteen story cement structure built by the Army as a barracks during WWII. The entire town lives in this building. Sectioned into hotel rooms, individual apartments, a general store, church, infirmary, post office, bar, and restaurant, it had everything you need. The cinder block walls gave the feeling of an army barracks.

After checking in and taking my gear to the room, spartanly furnished with a single bed, dresser, nightstand, toilet, and a small closet, I naturally gravitated to the bar.

The whole town seemed to have already congregated there for food and drink—mostly drink. Before long, the place got rowdy with dancing, singing, arguing, joke telling and arm wrestling. (The women usually won.) What else was there to do?

While warm and cozy inside, the nasty weather outside rattled the windows with blowing cold rain and fog. Hearing I was the weathered–in pilot, the locals came over to introduce themselves and welcome me to town. Most of the men had long hair and full beards. They dressed in dirty torn flannel shirts, jeans, and rubber boots. The women typically dressed the same, only with shorter beards. Just kidding.

A friendly bunch, especially later, after having way too much to drink, they had a little game of "swap room keys." Tossing their keys on the bar they randomly selected a key from the pile. After determining the key belonged to the opposite sex, that's who you went home with. Like I said—real friendly people.

Most of these folks were nice and friendly as can be, but not so good looking, and hairy—even the women, and big. The smell of unwashed bodies permeated the room. Most worked in the fishing industry and came directly to the bar after a long day and—well—you get the picture.

Fortunately, I had only consumed a few beers, as I had to fly in the morning. The crowd, getting a little too friendly for me, I managed to sneak up to my room without participating in their friendly game of key swap.

Early next morning, after a hearty breakfast, while visiting with a few of my "new best friends," I went outside to check the weather, and it had cleared considerably. I pumped the floats, did a cursory preflight and taxied out. I took off on the glassy water—like gliding across a mirror, without a breath of wind. I circled over the bay a few times to gain altitude before heading to the pass. A few clouds obstructed the first corner, but I was able to sneak back through partially clear skies to Anchorage.

Five days later I headed back to pick up the hunters, only to be turned back at the pass. I tried each day for the next three days, finding the pass socked in each time. I was usually the first one to try the pass in the morning, reporting conditions to Anchorage Flight Service as a PIREP (Pilot report of actual weather conditions in flight) to help other pilots. I burned lots of fuel during these attempts, but I needed to get my clients back.

After four days, I finally got through. The hunters met me at the airplane as I coasted into the beach. They were shaking their fists, bitching and whining at me for being late. I tried to explain the bad weather, but they didn't care. They were tired, dirty, and out of booze. We loaded up and headed for Anchorage. Guess what? The pass was socked in, so back to Whittier.

My hunters took their gear and boarded the train from Whittier to Anchorage which runs under Portage pass. I had to spend the night once again with my "way too friendly, new best friends."

This time, being somewhat more cautious, I took a few beers and a sandwich up to my room, skipping the bar scene. As a precaution, I double-bolted the door and put a chair against it. I left my 44-magnum pistol on my nightstand just in case one of these amorous, smelly, lady fishmongers decided to pay me a nocturnal visit.

I got back to Anchorage the next day, but it was still marginal getting through the pass.

I lost money on that trip.

Portage Pass looks pretty good on a clear day.

Chapter 14
Fred

While working on my helicopter rating in the Robinson R-22, flying up in the mountains behind Anchorage, I practiced pinnacle landings, confined area landings. I had some fun chasing Big Horn sheep up the side of the mountain, which is a real no-no, and just playing around getting comfortable with the helicopter. After about an hour of this fun and frivolity, I was headed back to the airport and noticed I was over the area where my old buddy Fred lived.

I had known Fred for 20 years. In all that time, I don't think I ever saw him when he wasn't stoned. He loved to smoke pot. His house was located deep in a forested mountainside behind Anchorage.

I thought I'd drop in and maybe take him for a ride. Hoping I could land in the little clearing in front of his house, I came in low, hovering in front of his second-story windows, trying to determine if the rotor blades would clear the trees for landing.

Dressed in my usual flying gear, baseball cap, radio headset, sunglasses and leather jacket, sitting alone in my Plexiglas bubble I hovered in front of his windows. I watched Fred running from one room to another carrying little bags. He seemed to be in a hurry and didn't look too happy. I hovered there for several minutes, and finally determined that I didn't have enough clearance to land. Nodding goodbye, I flew away.

Later that day, I called Fred to explain why I didn't land.

After calling me several nasty names, Fred explained, "I didn't recognize you, and I didn't know you were flying helicopters. I thought the state troopers were busting me, so I flushed all of my prime pot down the toilet."

I guess he finally had a day when he was not stoned.

***

The Cat Rescue
May 1974

My good friend Michael, a dentist in Anchorage, lived in Girdwood, about twenty miles from Anchorage. Girdwood had only one road, along the Turnagain Arm of Cook Inlet. The road runs along the water's edge on one side, with jagged, steep mountains on the other.

Michael was in town working when a huge avalanche blocked the road to Girdwood. Officials estimated it would take several days to clear the road. Michael called me, upset that his cat would run out of food and water. He asked if I would fly him out to pick up his cat.

I had been flying demonstration flights in the Aerospatiale Rally 235, a high-performance little aerobatic airplane, and decided to use this airplane for the rescue mission.

Girdwood had no airport, so we had to land on the highway. Numerous cars were parked along the road, with stranded motorists. I found a short stretch of highway with no cars and set the airplane down. I taxied back to the area with parked cars. People came running up to the airplane, hoping for a ride back to town. I explained I was on a "mercy mission" and couldn't take them on this flight. However, I would come back later. Michael hitched a ride to his house, returning a short time later with the cat.

A friendly state trooper blocked off enough of the road for me to take off.

Rescue accomplished, I made another five trips that day, hauling stranded people back to Anchorage. A very profitable day.

***

King Salmon
December 1980

A guiding service contracted me to fly supplies to the airport at King Salmon, 300 miles across the Wrangle Mountains from Anchorage. The day, although extremely windy and turbulent, at least had crystal clear visibility. King Salmon also had a massive, well-maintained runway used by large transport aircraft.

I flew my Cessna 185 on wheel skis. I had modified the airplane with a 'Robertson' STOL kit (Short Takeoff and Landing) which reduced the normal approach speed to 60 knots and lowered the stall speed and takeoff distance significantly.

During landing at King Salmon, I tried to hold 60 knots on approach to the runway, extremely challenging. I was violently tossed around by turbulence. When flaring for landing, as I slowed the airplane, something didn't look right in my peripheral vision out the side window. The runway was moving away from me, instead of towards me. The airplane was flying backward! My airspeed indicated fifty knots, but the wind was gusting down the runway to 70 knots. I finally got the plane down on the runway and had to literally fly it, on the ground all the way to the gas pumps. Fortunately, some people had been standing around watching my difficulties. They ran out to the airplane to help. I stayed in the cockpit with the engine running, brakes applied, using flight controls to hold the airplane in place while the helpers managed to grab the wing struts and get the airplane tied down for fueling.

Later I made the takeoff in about 20 feet.

***

Scatter the ashes
May 1980

One beautiful summer day, two middle-aged ladies came into the office to ask me if I would fly them over Mt. Susitna to scatter one of their husband's ashes. This mountain, nicknamed "Sleeping Lady" sat across Cook Inlet from Anchorage. Its profile looks like a sleeping lady; it's a beautiful mountain, and a lovely resting place for her husband's ashes. I felt this was to be a reverent event.

I loaded the ladies in the back seats and strapped the urn into the front right seat beside me. The "Sleeping Lady" was beautiful on this crispy cool summer day, still topped with a covering of snow and shimmering in the distance.

We flew around the mountain for some time until we found the perfect spot. The wife of the deceased said a few thoughtful words and a prayer, then asked me to scatter the ashes— a very touching moment. I opened the right side window, took the top off the urn as respectfully as possible, and then started pouring the ashes out the window.

Well...duh! All the ashes blew back inside the airplane into the faces of the two ladies in the back seat. I turned around, seeing their faces completely covered with ashes, except for the whites of their eyes.

All I could say was "Oops"! I absolutely couldn't help myself from laughing. They stared at me for a few seconds in shock. Then looked at each other, and they started laughing. We couldn't quit. We laughed all the way back.

Somehow I think the deceased husband would have gotten a laugh out of it and the wife probably giggles every time she looks across the bay to "Sleeping Lady."

It turned out to be a great "Celebration of life!"

Sleeping Lady

Chapter 15
Ferry flight to Fairbanks

October 1983

Working part time for an aircraft sales company in Anchorage, I had the opportunity to pick up and deliver many different types of aircraft in Alaska and beyond.

The company had just acquired an old Cessna 207 that had spent the last few years as a fish hauler, being flown off beaches, gravel bars, and dirt strips around Alaska, hauling fish from the nets located on the beaches.

This airplane needed to be flown from Anchorage to Fairbanks for the buyers. I needed to pick up a super cub on Fiber Floats in Fairbanks for the return trip to Anchorage.

The fish hauler was a sight: faded blue-and-white paint, scratched and dented. The horizontal stabilizer looked like someone had gone after it with a ball peen hammer. Dents and minor damage covered all the lower surfaces— damage obviously caused by years of operating on beach and gravel bars. I was surprised the prop gave any thrust at all after filing down so much. The tires were about half inflated and almost bald. The nose gear strut was flat, and the wing struts looked sandblasted.

Surrounding only one pilot seat, all the panels, headliner, and insulation had been removed to save weight. Fish guts, blood, scales, and other nasty looking stuff was splattered throughout the inside, even oozing from the seat tracks. It smelled so bad I had to leave the windows and doors open so that I wouldn't puke. I could barely see through the windscreen it was so scratched up and cloudy, even after a thorough cleaning and polishing.

The airplane had the basic instruments and one VHF radio. With any luck, this thing probably wouldn't start, and I wouldn't have to make the flight.

Anchorage to Fairbanks is 350 air miles with several mountain passes on the way, which could get iffy in bad weather. The weather this day was getting a little marginal, but still flyable.

I performed a very thorough preflight inspection, looking for any reason to cancel the flight. I determined, even though in pitiful shape, it was still flyable—barely.

To my surprise, the engine started right up, and the gauges displayed normal indications. Taxiing the airplane took an unusual amount of rudder and brakes to keep on the taxiway. This thing was a real piece of crap.

After struggling to the runway, I took off and turned north towards Fairbanks. Once in the air, it was almost impossible to keep flying straight without constantly holding rudder pressure.

The first few hundred miles were uneventful, except for a shaky leg from having to continually hold rudder pressure. As I entered the mountains, the cloud ceiling lowered, and it began to snow; then the winds kicked up causing turbulence and a very bumpy ride.

Once through the mountains, I called Fairbanks Tower. The radio went dead. I had a complete electrical failure—No navigation lights, no landing lights, and no wing flaps, as they were electric. *I should have expected it with this piece of crap!* Continuing, I did a fly-by over Fairbanks tower, wiggled my wings--standard procedure for radio failure--got the green light, came around and landed.

I taxied to the transient terminal and parked this junk heap where the new owner could find it. After scribbling a note with all the problems I had encountered, I tied the aircraft down and hitched a ride to the hotel.

Early the next morning, with much better weather, I took a taxi to pick up the super cub on floats. We had pre-arranged the pickup. The plane was there but there was no one to meet me at the aircraft. I had never flown a super cub and never heard of fiber floats. But how tough could it be?

Pre-flight inspection of this airplane showed the beautiful condition. I pumped out the floats, which were almost dry. After cranking up the little 150 horsepower engine, I taxied around a bit on the water to get the feel of the thing, while doing the checklist and run-up.

All was well. The radio even worked, although I wouldn't need it here, as I was on a lake outside Fairbanks. The weather was spectacular this day, and the little airplane a delight to fly. I made a few detours on the way home, landing at several tiny lakes just for the fun of it. I saw some moose and bears along the shorelines. After a beautiful flight back to Anchorage I landed on Lake Hood. What a sweet little airplane.

The following day I flew a Piper Turbo Saratoga out to a customer. I had never flown one of these. I had never even seen one before. I pulled out the operating manual, read how to fly it, and took off. Man, this thing was sweet. Plus it had plush leather interior, quiet, a total delight to fly.

You take the good with the bad in the airplane pick-up and delivery business.

Chapter 16
Ketchum Air Service

May 1983

Ketchum Air Service, the premier bush flying service, by far, in Anchorage, operated off Lake Hood with a fleet of two de Havilland Beavers, two Cessna 206 and one Cessna 185. They had been in operation at the same location for over twenty years. A family run business, the Ketchum's were the salt of the earth, no-nonsense, honest, hard-working people.

Marguerite and Ketch, the founders, were in their sixties at the time. Marguerite ran the office, scheduled the flights, and booked hotel rooms, transportation, and everything else related to getting the customers out to the airplanes. Still semi-active in the flying duties, Ketch kept his pilots in line. Craig, their son, also active in flying, took charge of maintaining the airplanes as well. During the busy flying months of summer, Ketchum hired three additional pilots, two mechanics, and half a dozen dock boys.

I had been flying in Alaska for over eight years and knew my way around pretty well. I had lots of experience in the Cessna 185 on floats, so when I read in the paper that Ketchum was looking for pilots, I applied. Old man Ketch personally gave the pilot interviews and grilled us! Finally, satisfied that we seemed to be knowledgeable, he said, "Put out your hands." He carefully examined our hands for calluses, indicating that we were also used to hard work.

Oddly enough, he never took us out for a check ride. I guess he figured if we got this far we must know how to fly. I felt honored to be one of the three chosen from over twenty applicants.

I didn't get to fly the airplane during my first week, even though I was in the air ten to twelve hours a day. Assigned to fly with Ketch in the 206, I operated the radios from the right seat, observing where he went, and how he operated the airplane. I took note of what power settings he used, landing approaches to the various lakes and rivers, and generally how he did things. The second week, Ketch put me in the left seat and told me to drive—and operate the radios. I felt successful when he fell asleep next to me. I figured he must trust me.

Back to the office, he told me I was on my own, gave me my next flight destination, and off I went. The following week we had a few hours of break time without passengers. Ketch told me to follow him out to the big De Havilland Beaver. Ketch got into the left seat to drive.

Off we went across Cook Inlet. Ketch told me to watch him carefully. He made several landings on the lake then shut off the engine. He told me to get over in the left seat. *Wow…I am going to fly this thing!*

There is only one set of controls in the Beaver, so when you've got it, you've got it! I was amazed at how easy the Beaver was to fly. The big Pratt & Whitney 985 radial engine pumps out 450 horsepower.

With no load, the airplane just jumped off the water. I came around, making several full stop landings and some step turns. Ketch said, "Take us back." That's all he said. I thought I did okay but didn't know what he was thinking.

When we got back to the dock, he said: "Put twenty gallons of fuel on board then go out and practice a while until you feel comfortable."

I'm on my own—alone! In a Beaver! A dream come true—wow—how many people get to fly one of these things?

I flew over to the same lake, shot a few takeoffs and landings and practiced some step turns. Everything felt really good, so I flew back. When I arrived at the dock, Ketch told me I had a group of passengers to fly up to Mt McKinley, in the other Beaver, already loaded and fueled. That was it! I was now a Beaver pilot!

We never knew what airplane we would be flying or where we were going on our next flight. As we pulled into the dock, the dock boys grabbed the airplane to tie it up. Craig or Ketch met us when we stepped out of the plane with our next destination marked on a map. The next airplane, a Beaver, a 206 or 185, already had been fueled up and loaded by the dock boys. All the pilot had to do was verify the proper fuel quantity, and off we went— a very efficient system and finely orchestrated by the Ketchum's.

During the long summer daylight, we flew as many as twelve or more hours each day. Ketch had some cots set up in a back room where we caught little naps during the day when we had time. It was a busy place.

Craig had a traditional way of finishing our long day. When we pulled up to the dock and climbed out for our next flight, he met us at the airplane with a "North Slope Special" as he called it—A tall double rum and coke! That declared the end of the day for flying and couldn't have tasted better.

As the salmon season approached, Ketch instructed all of us to keep an eye out to see where the fish came in. We used special code words to identify the lake or stream where we spotted salmon. All the operators used the same radio frequencies, and we didn't want the other guys to know where the fish were.

Ketchum had a special one-day Salmon fishing package: a one-day license, fishing pole, tackle box, hip-waders, and a box lunch.

He assigned me to a group of six Japanese passengers for the one-day fishing trip. We had spotted a lake where the salmon were running heavily. I flew the passengers over to the lake in the Beaver. I pulled the airplane up to the beach, then unloaded them and their gear. I lined them all up facing me.

The tourists all had their cameras hanging around their necks and wore white shirts, dress pants, hip wader boots, and baseball caps—quite a sight. Using one of the fishing poles, I demonstrated. They followed along with their gear, as I strung the line. I then took out a Pixy lure and hooked it to the line. Everyone paid rapt attention as they hooked up their Pixy's. I cast the Pixy into the lake, gave it a yank, and handed the bent-over vibrating pole with a salmon on it to one of the guys—*That* is how you catch a salmon!" Cheers went up all around as I bid them farewell, telling them I would pick them up in the afternoon.

I returned four hours later, finding they had so many fish I didn't think I could haul them all back. The tourists were grungy, dirty, and happy. Fortunately, the Beaver had very large compartments in the floats, and we were able to get everything back. We contacted the local meat processing company to prepare the fish for them.

I got a really big tip.

See the picture of the salmon on top of one float –

What am I going to do with all these fish?

Beaver on the dock at Ketchum's

Chapter 17
The Beaver

June 1983

While building hours and experience in the Beaver, the Ketchums gave me more challenges: heavier loads, external loads, even bulky loads that required flying with the rear doors removed. I could not believe it at times.

Arriving at the Beaver for my first flight of the day, I found 4x8 sheets of ¾ inch plywood stacked on top of the float spreader bars, all the way up to the bottom of the fuselage. The front right seat had been removed to make room for 2x4's that ran from the instrument panel all the way back through the rear baggage curtain and up to the headliner. Several large barrels of nails added to the mix. The airplane was so heavy the tops of the floats were almost awash.

The Beaver has a useful load of 2,000 pounds; I am sure we were way over.

It took an extremely long takeoff roll with a step turn at the end of Lake Hood for a longer run to get airborne. I had to cross my wake as I rolled one float out of the water to get the airplane in the air. Normal takeoff in the Beaver requires 10 degrees of flaps, which we retract in the climb. As I retracted the flaps, the airplane started to sink. I made the entire flight with the flaps at 10 degrees. Now *that* was a heavy load.

Another time, I strapped a boat to one side of the floats, 2x4's to the other side, and a bed with box springs and mattress on the inside. The box springs wouldn't fit inside the airplane, so the rear doors were removed. The box springs stuck out both sides of the airplane. It felt strange after takeoff. The box springs, being unstable, kept flexing back and forth in the wind, causing the airplane to feel like flying a rocking chair. I was glad to get that flight over.

Flying like this may seem extreme to most pilots in the lower forty-eight, but believe me, it was the norm in Alaska. If you didn't want to carry the full loads, then you didn't have a flying job. Someone was always willing to do it.

But I'm not saying I flew just *anything* without protest.

During another charter in a Seneca II, before hiring on at Ketchum's, as I walked toward the airplane, I saw it sitting on its tail, (not a tail-wheel airplane). The inside was full of heavy nitrogen bottles. As I climbed forward to the cockpit, the airplane rocked back down on its nose wheel. If I lost one engine on takeoff, with this load, the other engine would lead me to the scene of the crash. I told them, "No way," got out of the airplane, and then quit. Someone else took the flight. I like to fly, but I didn't have a death wish.

Another time I flew for a charter company in the Lake LA4-200 amphibian airplane. I had a full load of dynamite. They assured me the dynamite was safe, as long as there were no blasting caps. We'd make a separate flight with the caps. I took the flight, but was still nervous with this load. As I started getting into some light turbulence, I imagined seeing the oil pressure start to fluctuate, and the engine make strange noises.

Nothing was wrong with the airplane, just my imagination, as I worried about having to make an emergency landing with a load of dynamite. I successfully delivered my load.

Returning to Anchorage for the next load—blasting caps. They told me the guy that loaded my earlier flight had screwed up and also loaded the caps with the dynamite.

I quit!

* * *

During duck-hunting season at Ketchum's, we flew hunters to the duck flats across Cook Inlet from Anchorage. Duck flights were fun during low tide as we had to land the float planes on the mud. The mud was so slick and slimy that the floats slid along the mud and stopped. Then the Beaver would rock back on the heels of the floats—all very smooth.

For takeoff we had to steer the airplane with lots of power using the air rudder. Several landings and takeoffs created deep trenches in the mud. The airplane followed like it was almost on rails. The hard part was stepping off the floats and sinking up to your knees in the muck.

I made much longer trips through the Alaskan Range with heavy loads, flying out to the maximum range of the airplane. We carried extra five-gallon cans of fuel in the float compartments and had fuel caches hidden away at various locations if we were running a little dry. We always carried a funnel and chamois to filter any water from the fuel.

The most beautiful and most frightening flights for me were the "flightseeing" trips to Mount McKinley (Denali).

The glaciers and mountains around Mount McKinley are undoubtedly the most beautiful and awesome sights on the planet. The incredible size of the mountain is unbelievable. The mountains, glaciers, and valleys all seem so unbelievably big.

I usually had a full airplane, with four to six passengers. I flew across the Cook Inlet, up the Susitna River, keeping low at 1,000 feet, looking for moose and bear along the way. Reaching the mountains, we flew up Kahiltna Glacier, climbing 10 to 12,000 feet, flying between Mount Foraker (17,400 feet) on the left, and Mount Hunter (14,573 feet) on the right, up to the west buttress of Mount McKinley (20,230 feet). The supercharged Beaver could get up to about 13,000 feet on a good day.

The floor of the glacier in this area was 8,000 feet. If we were lucky, there were climbers on the mountain, the west buttress being the most popular route. On clear days, I rolled the airplane over on a wing tip, trying to glimpse the top of the mountain, thousands of feet above us. The mountain is so big it makes its own weather, the top usually obscured by clouds.

These flights were beautiful but frightening. It's hard to explain unless you have been there. Everything is so incredibly big you lose your perspective of size and depth. It felt like I was about to run into the side of the mountain when I was still a mile away. We weren't very high above ground level, but still over 12,000 feet above sea level where the airplane performance is sluggish. When the wind blows off the mountain, which it usually does, the ride got bumpy and felt very uncomfortable, with the slow control response of the airplane at this altitude.

Maybe I needed a head shrink because it always felt to me the mountain was alive— like it was a giant predator ready to grab and drag me into its bowels. Creepy!

In his book *"Wager the Wind"* Don Shelton describes landing his Super Cub at 14,500 feet on a snow patch on the side of Mount McKinley to make a rescue. I can't even imagine doing that.

As beautiful as it was, I felt extremely relieved to be out of there.

Leaving the mountain was the fun part. I descended to about 50 feet above the glacier, which glowed with beautiful turquoise pools of water, giant cracks, and crevasses. I followed its winding path down the mountain, descending from 8,000 feet at the top down to 1,500 feet.

Reaching the bottom of the glacier, making a slight detour around to the right—we landed on Chelatna Lake. I gave the passengers coffee, doughnuts, and a pee break, before our flight back to Anchorage.

Chelatna Lake is a beautiful alpine lake nestled in the mountains next to Kahiltna Glacier at 1,384 feet elevation. It is difficult to put into words the feelings I had while standing on this remote beach, viewing the grandeur of these giant mountains reflected in the mirror-like surface of the lake. One senses a feeling of total peace and solitude when standing in the presence of wild, profoundly beautiful scenery—to smell and feel the crispness of the fresh mountain air and hear the absolute total quiet.

Beaver flying near Mt. McKinley

Chapter 18
The Widgeon

September1983

A few months after getting my multi-engine seaplane rating in the Grumman Widgeon, my neighbor put his airplane up for sale. I negotiated a deal with him, and became the proud owner of this vintage WWII relic. This airplane is the same model of plane they flew in "Fantasy Island" when the little guy says, "da plane—da plane."

I intended to fly it commercially, as it could haul quite a load. The engines had been upgraded from the original Ranger engines, with fixed pitch props, to newer Continental 0-470 engines and constant speed props, giving much better performance.

Landing the airplane on water seemed almost too easy— just splash it down and it stayed there—as long as you were at the correct pitch attitude. Touching down too far forward on the hull caused the airplane to go into negative buoyancy, resulting in porpoising, (alternately rising and submerging, progressively getting worse) that could spoil your whole day if not immediately corrected. Taxiing on water was controlled with engine power and air rudder for steering.

Water takeoffs required pointing the airplane 90 degrees from the direction of takeoff, applying full power and full left rudder while turning to the direction of takeoff until coming on the step. This procedure kept water from hitting, and pitting, the props, while trying to avoid that nasty negative buoyancy, porpoising thing.

Landing the airplane on wheels was another matter, a total handful, requiring finesse and cajoling. The landing gear, close-coupled, (wheels close together) required the tail wheel to be locked in the center position for takeoff and landing. Crosswind landings required staggering the engine thrust, adding more power on the downwind engine and rolling the wing low into the wind. Then we cross-controlled the rudder to keep the nose pointed down the runway. After touching down we pushed the controls full forward to plant the airplane, then peddled the rudder back and forth to keep it straight until the tail came down, where the locked tail wheel stabilized the airplane.

Three point landings? Forget it!

Taxiing required an unlocked tail wheel, brakes, and engine power and air rudder to steer. It sounds difficult, but it wasn't that tough.

The airplane also had this little idiosyncrasy: occasionally when coming in for a landing, the wheels wouldn't all come down, indicated by a warning light in the cockpit. I carried a broom handle, which I used to poke down through the partition behind the pilot seat to reach the landing gear linkage and push it down to lock. Some of my passengers got concerned about this, but hey, it was an old airplane.

Flying by myself one day, just for fun, I decided to land at Big Lake Lodge for a hamburger, and, to show off my big twin engine seaplane.

After landing, I was taxiing past the lodge. I saw lots of people having lunch, watching me go by. They were probably thinking I was the coolest thing ever, driving this big twin engine seaplane. I had the cockpit side window open with my arm up on the sill, looking like a rock-star.

Located next to the restaurant was the boat ramp. I planned to taxi up the ramp into the parking area, spin around and shut down, then swagger into the lodge looking my dapper bush pilot self, my hat at a jaunty angle, ready to sign autographs. Maybe some hot babes would want an airplane ride.

Well, it didn't exactly work out that way. The boat ramp consisted of soft mud. As I gunned the engines to go up the ramp, the wheels dug into the soft mud and the airplane stopped dead, the nose burying itself in the muck with the tail sticking up in the air.

Now I had *everyone's* attention. Not the kind of attention I had planned on.

I shut down the engines as some people ran out to see if I needed help. I no longer felt like the dapper, hero, bush pilot, rock star. Mortified and embarrassed, my bubble burst, I just sat there red-faced and accepted help, noting a few grins and chuckles from the crowd.

Anyway, with lots of help, shovels, ropes, pushing and sweating, we finally managed to get the wheels out of the mud and the airplane back in the water. I never did get my hamburger.

Sometimes our egos need an attitude adjustment!

My Widgeon

Chapter 19
A Nasty Day

Having recently relocated to Sitka from Anchorage, I purchased a three-story log house in an area called Halibut Point on Baranof Island. Located about 50 feet from the water's edge, the house sat on a bank about 30 feet above sea level. The view was fantastic, looking out across the bay directly at Mt. Edgecombe, a semi-active volcano that occasionally spewed out smoke.

Hired by Mountain Aviation, a small air taxi operator, I flew out of Sitka airport. We operated two aircraft, a Cessna 185 and de Havilland Beaver, both on amphibious floats.

The amphibious floats gave us the option to land on water with the wheels retracted while also being able to use runways, gravel strips, and beaches. After the last flight of the day, on the way home, we landed in a freshwater lake and cycled the landing gear a few times to wash out the salt water. Back at the airport, we made one final wash-down with fresh water, spraying the wings, tail section, fuselage, and floats, to prevent salt water corrosion.

The following summer months I flew with Steve, the owner of the company. He sat in the right seat, teaching me my way around the area, using forest service maps and channel markers, positioned for ship navigation. Having no GPS back then, and the aircraft with only the basic instruments, we had to be thoroughly familiar with the channels, passes, canyons, and mountains.

Steve constantly asked me "Where are we? Show me on the chart."

Steve was a good teacher, and I quickly learned my way around. Although the summer weather was very mild, I couldn't understand why Steve insisted that I never fly more than 100 feet above the water, paying strict attention to the numbered channel markers.

He had me fly to channel marker number 15, then turn forty-five degrees right and start timing myself to marker 16, then turn right another fifteen degrees, hit the timer until reaching 17. Even though I could see the turns and knew where we were, he insisted on these procedures until I had it all down to memory. I also had to mark my forest service maps with the times, just in case. *I should have known what was coming.*

Winter approached, and the weather changed dramatically. Strong winds and rain developed with fog and low cloud ceilings. Occasionally, we had days of clear calm that were wonderful until interrupted by severe clear-air turbulence. I figured if it got too bad, we wouldn't fly. Was I ever wrong!

When the big Alaska Airlines 727 couldn't get into Juneau due to weather, they diverted to Sitka. A number of the passengers asked us to fly them to Juneau, under the ceiling at tree-top level through the passes, which got extremely exciting at times.

One time, BB King the blues singer, came off the 727 and someone brought him to our office for the continued flight to Juneau. He took one look at our airplane sitting on the ramp, and said, "No f...king way am I getting on that!"

He went back to the terminal to wait out the weather for the Alaska Airlines flight.

There was never a day when we didn't fly.

Walking out to the kitchen early one morning to get my coffee, I looked out the window and couldn't believe how bad the weather was. *No way, no one can fly in that.* Directly across the bay, the wind blew about 50 knots, and rain, with whitecaps, and blowing spray on the surface. Low clouds hung just above the sea—it was a nasty day!

Figuring this was going to be an easy day, I strolled into the office to relax with a cup of coffee, read the paper; maybe pull one of the airplanes into the hanger for some routine maintenance. In my dreams.

The minute I walked through the door, Steve told me "Get the Beaver fueled up; you have a pickup at Kake Village and then on to Angoon."

I pointed out the window. "Are you serious?"

"What? —a little rain and wind never hurt anyone." *Steve is obviously mentally unstable.*

The West side of Baranof Island, where we were located in Sitka, faces directly out to the Gulf of Alaska. Most of the villages where we flew were scattered throughout the myriad of islands and the mainland East of Baranof Island. If we had flights to the northeast of Baranof, we had to use the bays, inlets, and straits that separated Baranof from Chichagof Island. This was the Alaska Marine Highway with channel markers for navigation.

On flights southeast of Baranof, we had to use one of the passes through the mountains. We rarely had enough ceiling to fly directly over the 3,000 to 4,000 ft. mountains that blocked the center of the island. In all my time there I was able to fly over the top just once.

Kake was southeast, so I had to use the pass, which could be scary on a nasty day like this. It felt like I would be blown over just taxiing out to the runway. I did all my preflight run checks, hoping to find something wrong with the airplane so I wouldn't have to go. *Bummer—everything checks out okay.*

Roaring down the runway about 30 feet, I was airborne but flying sideways. Gear up flaps, up, prop and manifold pressure back to 20/20 as I headed out into the Gulf along the west, (windward side), of Baranof. I managed to get up to about 100 ft. before finding the solid cloud ceiling and had to drop down.

The plane was being tossed all over the place by the wind, the sea below me a maelstrom of waves, spray and, roiling water. The shoreline was nothing but jagged cliffs and rocks. *If the engine fails now, I will be history.* I headed south, keeping the Baranof shoreline off to my left, watching for the entrance to Whale Bay, which was about 40 miles south of Sitka. The rain poured so hard I could barely see past the prop.

The pass I looked for is called Whale Bay/Gut Bay. Whale Bay is several miles wide at the mouth and runs back about five miles into the mountains. It then funnels down to about one-half mile wide for another several miles and stops. At this point, I had to find the low pass through the mountains. This pass narrows down to barely two wingspans and runs for about five miles. Vertical cliffs soar up several thousand feet on both sides; then it opens up to Gut Bay, then to Chatham Strait.

Wide Whale Bay narrows down to a mountain pass, then opens to wide Gut Bay—a perfect venturi—like the carburetor on an engine that is designed to accelerate the air flow. The wind blew about 40 to 50 knots when I entered Whale Bay. This meant it was blowing probably 60 to 80 knots in the pass. It made for an extremely exciting ride.

Entering the narrow section, I always tried to stay to the right, as there was barely enough room for two aircraft to pass in opposite directions. Keeping to the extreme right also gave me a look down the pass to see if it was weathered in. If I couldn't see through the pass, I continued the turn, with just enough room to turn around at this spot only. Once into the pass, I was committed.

Turning into the narrow section, I could see through the pass. All was clear, so I continued. Suddenly, it felt like a giant hand grabbed the airplane, shaking it like a rag doll. It tossed me around so violently I could hardly keep my eyes in focus. My seat belt strapped me tight to the seat, but my upper body was slammed into the side door, then into the control yoke so hard I feared I would break something. It was all I could do to keep the top of the glare shield level with the horizon. The roll rate of the winds and turbulence exceeded the roll rate of the flight controls, and I was just along for the ride. *This shit is scary! It feels like the plane will start coming apart.*

I was being tossed up, rolled over to where the wing tip was pointing ninety degrees straight down, then hammered from below—then kicked in the side. *This is it. I will become a splat on the face of the cliffs.* And then I was out of it, into Gut Bay.

Flying into Chatham Straight, I turned north. The wind died down, and the ceiling lowered to about 50 feet, with the rain coming down in sheets. I dropped down to just above the water, continuing north, looking for the channel marker for Fredrick Sound.

The ceiling continued to lower down to the water. I pulled back the power and landed on the relatively smooth sea. I kept enough power to keep the airplane on the step, maintaining about 40 knots airspeed. I followed my compass heading for several miles until the ceiling lifted enough for me to take-off again. I flew very low above the water, when directly ahead of me, out of the rain and fog, materialized a fishing boat with a tall mast—*Oh shit!*

I pulled back hard on the control wheel and shot up into the clouds, just clearing the mast. That woke me up!

In the clouds with zero visibility, I slightly recovered my senses. Although I had an instrument rating, the airplane didn't. I tried to keep the wings level with my artificial horizon indicator while descending to where I could see again.

I found the channel marker, flew around the corner and landed at Kake. As I picked up my passengers, they asked, "How was the weather coming over?"—"Oh, nothing unusual," I told them. "Just another nasty day."

Then we had to fly back through it all.

Chapter 20
The Goat Hunt

By late October, the temperature dropped, and snow dusted the mountain tops. Goat hunting season had arrived. I was busy flying hunters to remote locations. I dropped the hunters off, and came back a few days or a week later to pick them up. Hopefully, they had trophies to bring home.

A group of hunters arrived, dressed in brand new hunting regalia: bright-colored waterproof down jackets, pants, hats, and shiny new mountain-climbing boots. The hunters, all in their mid-thirties, looked fit. Carrying high powered telescope rifles stored in hard cases they insisted we handle with care. One large bright-colored tent, sub-zero sleeping bags, a case of food, several cases of beer a bottle of Jack Daniels, and a ten-pound bag of salt to treat the hides. As Alaska residents from Anchorage they were not required to have a hunting guide, as is the case for non-residents.

Their destination was Rosenberg Lake, high in the mountains behind Sitka, a great hunting location, as it provided good access to Mt. Rosenberg and the higher elevations of Baranof Island, with a large population of mountain goats. Less than 20 miles North of Sitka, this lake was one of my most feared places to fly. Naturally, I got assigned the flight.

I flew straight off the end of the runway for about ten miles, then turned up Nakwasina Sound, climbing in altitude. About five miles up the bay, the ocean water ended on the face of the mountains. Rosenberg Lake, located at 2,500 feet elevation in the bowl of a small box canyon is surrounded by 1,000 foot cliffs on all sides except, one. It had a narrow opening where I entered and departed—one way in and one way out.

The lake is approximately 300 feet wide by 2,600 feet long with steep cliffs jutting up at forty-five-degree angles from the water's edge. A dramatic waterfall rushed out the open end, dropping almost 2,000 feet off the face of the cliff.

The winds usually blew off the Gulf into the box canyon, hitting the back wall, twisting and turning in unpredictable directions. In really windy conditions, we just couldn't fly in there. Even on good days I never really knew what to expect once I entered the canyon.

I did my usual approach for landing, flying through the narrow opening, then alongside the right side of the lake as close to the cliffside as possible. Once reaching the end of the canyon, I chopped the power, pumped down the flaps, pointed the nose steeply down, kicked hard rudder, and rolled the wing tip over. This put the airplane in an extreme slip, sliding sideways down the face of the mountain to the water. Just above the lake, I straightened everything out and lined up for touchdown. Once the floats touched the water, I pushed hard forward on the controls so the float tips would help slow the airplane.

As expected, the winds turned around to hit me on the tail during landing, and the lake being so short, made it difficult to stop. That was the easy part. After landing, the passengers didn't say a word. They had that "deer in the headlights" look on their faces for a few seconds, then they cheered and clapped.

Most non-pilots have never experienced an extreme slip down the face of a cliff, but it was the only way to keep the airspeed slow enough while rapidly descending, and allowed me to utilize most of the lake for landing. A normal approach to landing would never work in a place like this.

We taxied back to a small beach at the far end of the lake where I shut down the engine and coasted onto the sand. Jumping into the shallow water wearing my hip waders, I grabbed a float, spun the airplane around, and pulled the heels of the floats onto the beach where the passengers could walk off the back. After unloading passengers and gear they were enthusiastic to set up camp in this magnificent alpine setting

I usually left the hunters from four to six days. We scheduled a pickup date, but I explained we had to be flexible, depending on the weather.

The airplane was light, and take-off was no problem.

The time came to pick up the hunters and their trophies. Flying them out is where it got interesting!

On this particular trip, I was late for the pickup by a few days due to strong winds blowing off the Gulf of Alaska. I finally had to go for the pickup, even though the winds had calmed down only slightly. When I landed at Rosenberg, the wind blew so hard on my tail, I used most of the lake to get stopped.

The hunters had been out a week, as planned, and three days more, due to wind and weather. They were not in a good mood.

A soggy, grimy mess, with torn, blood-and-mud-stained clothing, the hunters sported eight-day beards and smelled really bad, like a bouquet of unwashed bodies, bad breath and wet goats. They had run out of beer and Jack Daniels and were pissed I was late. I tried to explain how dangerous this place was to fly in or out of when the wind and weather were bad. They acted like I was making excuses.

They had indeed been successful; they all had goats. Everyone brought back their complete animals, hides, heads and all the precious meat. I figured I could still get off with everything in one trip, so we loaded up their gear and trophies. I ran out of room inside the airplane and had to stow the goat meat in float compartments.

The tail winds still blew slightly beyond my comfort zone, so these guys would soon see what I was talking about when we made our take-off.

I turned the Beaver around, pulling the heels of the floats up on the sandy beach. Everyone got strapped in as I cranked up the engine. I set the flaps and trim for takeoff, letting the oil temp warm up. I needed all the power of the 450 HP supercharged engine.

During a slight lull in the wind, I announced, "here we go" I gave the engine full power, and we sluggishly started to move. We were heavy, I could feel it was taking much longer than normal to accelerate and come up on the step. The wind was again gusting on my tail.

Finally, we were on the step, the airplane slowly gaining airspeed as we headed towards the waterfall at the end of the lake. On and on we went —I was running out of lake and it looked like I wasn't going to make it. The end of the lake closing fast and I still wasn't at flying speed. With no way to stop or turn, I was committed. I reached the end of the lake, still on the water. Desperately, giving the flaps one more pump, I rolled one float out of the water and yanked back hard on the control wheel. The airplane came out of the water a few feet, and we sailed over the waterfall, losing all ground effect. The airplane began to shudder, almost breaking into a stall. I shoved the nose hard over, pointing down almost vertical, looking out the forward windscreen I could see the jagged rocks 2,000 feet below. Slowly I felt the heavy airplane respond and gain airspeed. I eased back on the controls to gently recover from the dive and level out.

A quick glance over my shoulder showed my passengers wide eyed and green, shaking from their harrowing takeoff. The stayed silent, not saying a word the rest of the way home.

And me? —I was shaking so hard I could hardly hold my double rum and coke back at the airport!

If I had my choice today of flying into that lake or getting a root canal, I would be on my way to the dentist!

The Beaver on amphibian floats at Sitka airport

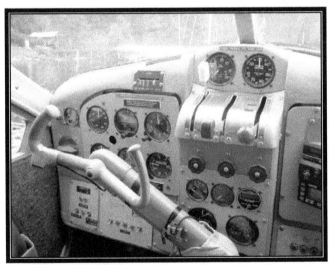

Beaver instrument panel—minimal

Chapter 21
Fog and Glassy Water

A beautiful day for flying: calm wind, clear skies, and no turbulence. I was to fly a Fish and Game guy to one of their remote facilities, located on the east side of Baranof Island, just inland off Chatham Straight.

This time I was flying the Cessna 185 on amphibian floats. We took off from Sitka Airport flying south along the west (seaward) side of Baranof Island. Reaching the entrance to Whale Bay we turned east, flying over the bay, a right turn at the end of the bay took us through the pass to Gut Bay, then out over Chatham Straight.

Having never been to our destination lake, the Fish and Game guy was giving me directions. We flew north, passed Hoggatt Bay, then turned into a small canyon where he said "The lake should be in about a mile, once around the corner to the right, you should start letting down."

As I turned the corner, I saw the lake, at least part of the lake. I could only see about 100 yards of glassy water. Fog obscured the rest. The Lake, about a mile long with towering mountains on both sides, had no place for me to turn around. Turning over glassy water at low altitude is something one does not do. I was committed.

I lined up as best I could over the lake while trying to keep the shoreline in sight for depth perception. Landing on glassy water is like landing on a mirror—you can't tell your distance from the water. I held the nose up in the landing attitude and tried to maintain a 200 foot per minute descent on my vertical speed indicator. I knew the lake was short. I entered the fog. Seeing nothing but grey outside the airplane, I tried to keep the wings level using my instruments while descending. I worried about running off the end of the lake and unconsciously eased back on the controls. The airplane ran out of airspeed and stalled at five feet above the water, dropping like a rock. We hit so hard my seat broke and collapsed out from under me; I felt a pain in my back as I hit the floor. Pulling the power back to idle I tried to determine our damage, and if we were going to stay afloat. We slowly taxied through the dense fog and smooth water, finally sighting the indistinct outline of the shore, I shut down the engine, and we coasted in.

I struggled out of the cockpit, my back in real pain. After catching my breath, the pain eased up enough that I was able to wade around and inspect the airplane for additional damage. Fortunately, the broken seat seemed to be the only problem. I could fly from the other seat.

The Fish and Game guy was okay, and he understood what happened. That was the hardest landing I had ever made! After a few hours, the fog lifted enough for me, to take-off. I climbed into the right seat and bid farewell to my passenger. The return flight was smooth air all the way, which was good as I still worried about airplane damage.

Once back in Sitka I pulled the airplane into the hanger and did a thorough inspection, finding no damage except for the seat—and my back. I straightened a few bent parts on the seat, put some heat on my back, and all was well. Glassy water, fog, short unfamiliar lake—bad combination. I was lucky!

Chapter 22
Medivac

June 1984

On this cold, rainy, windy day, the weather remained so bad no one was flying, not even the birds around the airport. The boss was out of town, and I had just finished doing a brake job on the Cessna 185 in the hangar. I strolled into the office for a cup of coffee as the phone rang.

An accident had happened at the sawmill east of Baranof Island. One of the men needed urgent medical attention and evacuation. I explained the weather was too bad for flying, but I would try when it cleared up a bit. They insisted that he needed *urgent* evacuation or he might not survive. I told them I would call back in a few minutes. I contacted the local medic, explaining the situation, and asked if he would be willing to fly with me if I gave it a try. He immediately agreed, saying he would head out to the airport right away.

I called the saw mill, telling them "I'll try to get there, but it's doubtful."

The medic arrived within twenty minutes. We removed the rear seats from the Beaver to make room for a stretcher. The howling wind and rain almost blew us off our feet as we untied the aircraft from the ramp.

Soaked to the skin, shaking from the cold, we finally got on board. It was all I could do to control the airplane on the ground as we taxied out to the runway. I literally had to fly the airplane on the ground. Sitka flight service told us we were crazy to fly in this weather. Hey, a guy's life's at stake—we had to try. I completed a

121

quick run up, and we rolled out for takeoff. In seconds we were airborne; the airplane turned almost sideways, weathervane into the gusting wind.

We flew south alongside the island, trying to keep ground reference out my side window, as visibility out the front windscreen was almost nil. The wind tossed us around as if being in a clothes dryer, weightless one second, pulling several G's the next. No way could I even keep the wings level in the maelstrom. The sea below churned in a mayhem of crashing waves and whitecaps. Survival would not have been possible if the engine failed and we had to land.

After 35 miles of adrenalin rush, we found the entrance to Whale Bay-Gut Bay pass. The turbulence and rain became even worse here; it almost slammed us into the cliffs. Exiting the pass, we dropped down just above the water and flew across Chatham Strait to Hamilton Bay where the sawmill was located. We flew at 50 feet altitude to maintain ground (water) visibility. The landing was bumpy and rough due to the churning, roiling white-capped waters, gusting winds, and blinding rain. As we taxied in, several workers ran to the airplane to help secure us to the dock.

Another group of men carried the patient out to the airplane on a stretcher. He was indeed in a bad way and only semiconscious. We secured the stretcher to the floor in the back where we had removed the seats and strapped the patient in.

The medic immediately checked the patient's vitals and overall condition. He discovered a possible broken back and numerous other injuries. He started an IV as I cranked up the engine. The guys gave us a push-off, and I fought to get turned into the wind. Waves and blowing rain tossed us around like a toy boat. The waves almost buried the floats, and the torrential rain obstructed forward visibility. The perfect storm.

The takeoff was rough in the churning waters. With no forward visibility, I had to feel and hear the takeoff rather than see it. I became *one* with the airplane. I sensed the subtle pressure changes in the controls through my arms, heard the slight variations of engine pitch, felt the pressure of the floats struggling across the unfriendly surface. I was in my element, not reacting to conscious thoughts—just doing, being, becoming. I *was* the airplane. I instinctively knew when to lift-off.

I used skills and intuition developed over thousands of hours flying float planes, I was in control.

We lifted off the tossing sea. I had just pumped up the flaps, fighting the controls, when the medic yelled "hold this" and thrust me the IV bag. I controlled the yoke (pitch and roll) with my knee, the throttle and prop with my left hand, one foot for the rudder pedals, while I clutched the IV bag in my right hand. I was flying in conditions no sane person would attempt. I didn't know what I would do if had to scratch an itch. *I can do this, I am in control.*

The medic had his problems, with only a makeshift seat belt, he had to sit on the floor as he tended to his patient, and tried to hang on through this roller coaster ride.

The trip home was just as bad, but we made it, and the guy survived. I logged 3.9 hours of unmitigated fear on that trip.

A calm, quiet desk job might be nice.

Chapter 23
Open Ocean Landing

October 1984

My mission that day was to fly a crew member and supplies to a crab fishing boat. The uncommon thing about this flight: I had to meet the boat at sea, landing in the open ocean approximately ten miles west of Cape Spencer in the Gulf of Alaska.

With clear skies on a cool and sunny day we flew out of Sitka. The de Havilland Beaver leisurely climbed to a cruise altitude of 4,000 feet, the big radial engine producing a powerful, satisfying rumble. I leveled off heading north. We followed the shoreline for the next hundred miles, enjoying the smooth flight and clear skies.

Reaching Cape Spencer, about forty miles west of Juneau, I turned toward the open ocean on a 240 degree heading. It felt wrong: Deliberately flying out to sea in a single engine airplane, planning to land in the open ocean. *Do I need a reality check?*

I called the boat on a predetermined VHF radio frequency. Using their DF (Direction Finding) receiver, they gave me an inbound bearing to fly until we visually sighted the vessel.

I let down to 1,000 feet as we searched for the little boat in the great big sea. It seemed like we flew forever before finally spotting it, gently rising and falling in the swells. The swells ran about four to five feet high, with 10 to 15 knot winds blowing directly with the swells, white capping off the crests.

These conditions convinced me there was no way I could land into the wind, directly into the swells—that would probably sink the airplane. I had to land parallel to the swells.

Flying float planes in Alaska for ten years, accumulating over 3,000 hours, I had never made an open ocean landing. No one had briefed me on the correct procedures. I was on my own!

Visualizing a runway with five-foot humps down the middle—the airplane skipping over one hump then crashing into the next. No, that wouldn't work.

With only one chance to do this right, even the slightest screw-up would turn me into nothing more than an oil slick with bits and pieces floating on the surface. I was scared!

The wind and swells came from the west, which required me to land in a northerly direction, the wind 90 degrees off my left wing tip.

Focusing my total concentration on the approach, I flew as slow as possible with full flaps, carrying power all the way. I aimed for the top of a swell, trying to touch down on the left float. *I am in the zone.*

Gently touching down, my left wing low into the wind, I skimmed along the crest of a swell, cross-controlling with the rudder to keep the airplane straight, then pulled back engine power. I kept the wing low. The floats slid off the swell to the side, into the trough then up onto the next swell as I slowed down and stopped. I bobbed in the ocean like a toy. *Wow, that is a new experience!*

Adding power, I slowly taxied over to the boat, where a crew member threw over fenders. I shut down the engine and coasted up as he grabbed the wing, pulled us in, and tightly secured the airplane to the rail.

Deathly quiet surrounded me after shutting down the big engine. The airplane and boat rose and fell as one in the sea. The sea gently lapped at the floats as my passenger quickly offloaded his supplies and gear and then jumped over to the boat. I never left the pilot seat. The captain offered me the biggest king crab leg I had ever seen; it was at least two feet long. "Here," he said, "something to munch on during your flight home."

They untied the airplane and pushed me off. *I feel so small, in this great big ocean .* I cranked up the engine and tried to determine the best way to take off. It had to be the same as the landing. No screw-ups allowed. *I am scared shitless!*

With a direct crosswind from my left, I applied full power as the aircraft was just rising to the top of a swell. As I accelerated, the airplane slid into a trough and then up on top of the next swell. I continued to keep a wing low into the wind while I applied opposite rudder to keep going straight (similar to my landing). On the crest of the third swell, I finally got airborne, let out a sigh of relief, and turned directly for the shoreline and home.

The water temperature was below 40 degrees. I wouldn't have survived long if I'd gone in.

I will never—ever—do that again!

Just recently I checked with an Air Taxi operator in Alaska, and they adamantly informed me, "We don't do that!"

Chapter 24
Leaving Sitka

October 28 1985

The extreme flying conditions were starting to get to me. Most days it was a challenge just to get back home alive.

Maybe it all started the day turbulence was so bad it popped a few rivets from the wings and the rear seat popped loose from the floor to fly up and smack me in the head. Perhaps it was a proverbial paradigm shift that the thrill was gone, or maybe I was just scared. But I was done.

I was done...

...flying an airplane that was almost as old as me, through severe turbulence that felt like it could rip the wings or tail off.

...flying through rain squalls so thick I couldn't see through the windscreen and had to look out the side window for reference.

...flying fifty feet off the water to stay below the cloud ceiling and landing in choppy seas when the visibility went to zero.

...trying to takeoff with the aircraft so heavy it wouldn't fly until removing fifty pounds of weight and wallowing into the air.

...flying in and out of lakes that were too small to operate a floatplane and only possible by using all the tricks in the book I had learned in over 4,000 hours of flight

...flying through mountain passes in foggy, cloudy conditions where mostly sheer luck got me through.

...flying over mountains in such windy condition that the mountain wave effects tried to suck me into the cliffs.

...landing in open ocean swells that no one in their right mind would do.

...taking off and landing in narrow streams around corners where logs or rocks could have taken me out in a heartbeat.

...landing at short dirt strips, dozed-out of the hillsides for mining operations, with tall mountains and no possible go around.

...falling through the ice with the airplane on skis.

...falling through deep powder in subzero weather, and spending days to dig out.

...landing among icebergs that calved off glaciers.

...dragging a wing tip while landing in cross winds that far exceeded the aircraft limits.

...flying way over gross weight with the doors removed.

...flying dynamite and caps on the same flight.

...flying medivac in weather where no one else would fly, to save a life.

...flying through snow and ice storms where the airplane got so heavy it almost would not fly.

* * *

Having pushed the airplanes and myself to the limits for the last twelve years, I was finally finished. Done!

Figuring I had used up my nine lives, I was starting to dread the flights. I just didn't want to do it anymore.

I was one of the lucky ones--I survived. Several of my bush pilot friends didn't make it.

Trading my last airplane, a Lake Buccaneer, for a sail boat in San Francisco Bay, I gave my notice and moved aboard my boat, a 32-foot Westsail.

I got a part time job flying the sea plane out of Sausalito. It was a Cessna 172 on floats...scenic flights over San Francisco, Alcatraz Island, Seal Rocks and the Golden Gate Bridge.

We only flew in clear, calm weather. What a change. It actually got kind of boring, except for the times my back seat passengers decided to join the mile high club.

* * *

Those 12 years were an adventure that most people can't even begin to imagine—experiences beyond my wildest dreams as a pilot.

I saw the incredible, raw beauty of magnificent towering mountains, pristine alpine lakes and wilderness streams teeming with fish.

I witnessed the unbelievable beauty of the northern lights over a frozen landscape, and the absolute absence of sound while standing on a remote beach, miles from another human.

I waded up streams in knee-deep waters where the salmon were so thick that I barely missed stepping on them with each stride.

I wandered across the seemingly boundless red and gold-colored Alaskan tundra, with not a tree in sight, savoring juicy wild blueberries that grew as far as the eye could see.

I relished the smell of a campfire while sitting around it with big game hunters from around the world, drinking really bad coffee.

I reveled in landing a float plane on a quiet, unnamed lake on a warm summer evening, solely to watch the moose and bear graze along the shoreline, and marveled at the splendor around me.

I felt in awe at flying up-close to Mt. McKinley and experiencing the absolute enormity of the mountain that is so immense that it makes its own weather, and conversely, the absolute terror when the mountain winds whipped-up, seemingly wanting to drag me into its bowels.

I was truly honored to get to know the Alaskan "bush" people, to fly with them, to be weathered-in with them, and especially to call them friends.

I was privileged to fly with, and learn from, those who I consider to be the best pilots in the world. Sadly, some didn't make it. I was one of the lucky ones.

My life is made rich with these memories, (and I actually relived a few while writing this book).

* * *

Acknowledgments

I would like to thank the many people who encouraged and helped me get the stories from my pilot log book into this book.

The La Mesa creative writing class which was almost too critical at times, but taught me how to write.

Linda Smith for her editing and advice.

Maureen Austin for her wonderful front and back cover designs in addition to her creative suggestions.

My many friends who read my first drafts and commented.

My wife Mendi who never stopped encouraging me to keep going and finish the book.

Thank you all…I could not have done it alone.

—Lynn Wyatt

About the Author

Lynn Wyatt learned to fly in Santa Monica, California.

But where he *REALLY* learned to fly was in the Alaskan bush country, the ultimate in wilderness and weather extremes.

The planes he flew ranged from Cessna 150's and Piper Champs to the iconic De Havilland Beaver and multi engine seaplanes

The cargo he carried included everything from basic supplies to full-sized mattresses with the airplane doors removed and to boats strapped to the outside of the plane for those living off the grid. His passengers ran the gamut of city-slickers wanting a "wilderness experience" to an accident victim who would have died had he not risked his own life to fly the man for medical attention.

It was no job for sissies. After 12 years and multiple near-death experiences, Lynn finally hung up his bush pilot wings.

He spent a short time flying sea planes out of Sausalito before moving to Los Angeles to work for Flying Tigers as an engineer, and then to San Diego where he spent the next 20 years with United Technologies Aerospace Systems (UTAS).

Upon retirement, he briefly worked as a flight instructor at Gillespie Field in El Cajon, California, until being asked to return to UTAS, where he still works part time, supporting the engine development program at NASA space center in Stennis, Mississippi.

His ratings include ATP (Airline Transport Pilot, SEL (Single Engine Land), SES (Single Engine Sea), MEL (Multi Engine

Land), MES (Multi Engine Sea, AGI (Advance Ground Instructor), CFI (Certified Flight Instructor), A&P (Airframe & Power plant Mechanic.)

Lynn currently lives with his wife, Mendi, and their cat, Abby, in a Mediterranean-style home high on a hill east of San Diego, California, with a view to the ocean, over 30 miles away.

His hunt for Alaskan big game has been replaced with diligent surveillance for the abundant native rattlesnakes that slither around his home. (To date, he has found 21 on his property.)

And his appetite for high-flying planes has now been exchanged for road-hugging Jaguar cars and his special Aston Martin.

Lynn Wyatt

CPSIA information can be obtained
at www.ICGtesting.com
Printed in the USA
LVHW040725191218
600890LV00001B/85/P

9 781634 926973